Ethical Insight, Ethical Action: Perspectives for the Local Government Manager

The International City Management Association is the professional and educational organization for chief appointed management executives in local government. The purposes of ICMA are to enhance the quality of local government and to nurture and assist professional local government administrators in the United States and other countries. In furtherance of its mission, ICMA develops and disseminates new approaches to management through training programs, information services, and publications.

Managers, carrying a wide range of titles, serve cities, towns, counties, and councils of governments in all parts of the United States and Canada. These managers serve at the direction of elected councils and governing boards. ICMA serves these managers and local governments through many programs that aim at improving the manager's professional competence and strengthening the quality of all local governments.

The International City Management Association was founded in 1914; adopted its City Management Code of Ethics in 1924; and established its Institute for Training in Municipal Administration in 1934. The Institute, in turn, provided the basis for the Municipal Management Series, generally termed the "ICMA Green Books."

ICMA's interests and activities include public management education; standards of ethics for members; the *Municipal Year Book* and other data services; urban research; and newsletters, a monthly magazine, *Public Management,* and other publications. ICMA's efforts for the improvement of local government management—as represented by this book—are offered for all local governments and educational institutions.

D1446061

PRACTICAL MANAGEMENT SERIES JAN 1990

Ethical Insight
Ethical Action

Perspectives for the Local Government Manager

ed by
Kellar

IA

PRACTICAL MANAGEMENT SERIES
Barbara H. Moore, Editor

The Practical Management Series is devoted to the
presentation of information and ideas from diverse
sources. The views expressed in this book are those of
the contributors and are not necessarily those of the
International City Management Association.

Library of Congress Cataloging-in-Publication Data

Ethical insight, ethical action: perspectives for the local
  government manager/edited by Elizabeth K. Kellar.
    p. cm.—(Practical management series)
    Bibliography: p.
    ISBN 0-87326-053-8
    1. Local government. 2. Political ethics. I. Kellar, Elizabeth
K., 1948- . II. International City Management Association.
III. Series.
JS155.E84 1988
352′.00047—dc19   88-8932
                                                      CIP

Printed in the United States of America.
9392919089
5432

Foreword

Local government managers perceive ethics as central to public service, and they have demonstrated a longstanding interest in a publication that would explore this important aspect of their work and their lives. Understanding—and acting on—clearly articulated ethical beliefs is one of the most powerful ways to ensure the survival of democratic ideals.

There is perhaps a tendency in management education to focus on the "hard" aspects of management such as financial analysis and engineering. This volume underscores the importance of the human dimension of management. The book covers the inevitable tensions between personal and organizational ethics, and several of the articles deal specifically with the nature of responsibility in public organizations. Managers are offered a number of practical, specific suggestions for evaluating their own ethical patterns or those of others; determining the ethical implications of decisions; and establishing procedures and programs that will make ethics an integral part of organizational life. A special section on codes of ethics includes a detailed argument in support of codes, as well as examples of ethical dilemmas managers are likely to face.

This book is part of ICMA's Practical Management Series, which is devoted to serving local officials' needs for timely information on current issues and problems.

We are grateful to Elizabeth K. Kellar for organizing and compiling the volume and to Sandy Chizinsky Leas for her research and editorial guidance in developing the book. Special thanks also to Bayard Catron of George Washington University for his assistance and encouragement in planning this volume. We wish also to thank the individuals and organizations that granted ICMA permission to reprint their material.

William H. Hansell, Jr.
Executive Director
International City
Management Association

About the Editor and Authors

Elizabeth K. Kellar is Associate Director of ICMA and the staff advisor to ICMA's Committee on Professional Conduct. She has made presentations on ethics at ICMA's annual conference and at state and regional ICMA meetings. In 1987, Ms. Kellar developed a guidebook on ethics for state training programs and wrote the handbook for *The Ethics Factor*, an ICMA training package for local governments. Ms. Kellar has edited another ICMA publication, *Managing with Less*, and coedited *Effective Communication: Getting the Message Across*. Ms. Kellar was formerly community relations officer of Sunnyvale, California, has served as an instructor for the National Training and Development Service, and was a member of the Montgomery County, Maryland, Commission on the Future. Ms. Kellar has a master's degree in journalism and political science from Ohio State University.

Following are the affiliations of the contributors at the time of writing:

James S. Bowman, Florida State University, Tallahassee, Florida.

G. Curtis Branscome, City Manager, Decatur, Georgia, and former Vice-President for the Southeast Region, ICMA Executive Board.

George Adrian Hayhurst Cadbury, chairman, Cadbury Schweppes PLC.

Ralph Clark Chandler, associate professor of political science and staff member, Center for Public Administration Programs, Western Michigan University, Kalamazoo, Michigan.

Saul W. Gellerman, Dean, University of Dallas Graduate School of Management.

Kristine R. Hanson, co-author with Robert C. Solomon of *Above the Bottom Line*, a textbook in business ethics.

Clark Moeller, president, Moeller Associates, management consultants, Towanda, Pennsylvania.

Mark Pastin, professor of management and director of the Center for Ethics, Arizona State University, Tempe, Arizona.

Frank P. Sherwood, founding director, University of Southern California Washington Public Affairs Center, Washington, DC.

Robert C. Solomon, professor, University of Texas at Austin and co-author of *Above the Bottom Line.*

Debra W. Stewart, associate professor of political science and public administration and associate dean of the graduate school at North Carolina State University, Raleigh, North Carolina.

Dennis F. Thompson, professor of politics, Princeton University, Princeton, New Jersey.

Revan A. F. Tranter, executive director of the Association of Bay Area Governments, Oakland, California, and chair, ICMA Committee on Professional Conduct.

York Willbern, emeritus professor of public and environmental affairs and political science, Indiana University, Bloomington, Indiana.

Douglas T. Yates, Jr., associate professor of organization and management and political science, Yale University, New Haven, Connecticut.

Contents

Introduction

G. Curtis Branscome

The concern with ethics, with a code of behavior or a set of values to guide our choices about behavior, has been a concern ever since the human race had the luxury of making choices. Ethics as a discipline or a matter for formal study entered what came to be called "Western civilization" with the early Greeks. Socrates has been described as "the first ethicist."[1] While the predominant view inherited from ancient Greece held that the best behavior was that which was consistent with reason, there were competing value systems. These ranged from Epicureanism, which held that the greatest good was obtained by the pursuit of personal pleasure, to Stoicism, which held that the greatest good was obtained through passive acceptance and freedom from passion.

Ethicists of many different traditions have influenced Western civilization. Jesus of Nazareth gained a following while espousing radical values and simple rules of behavior. That the meek, downtrodden, and poor might be blessed was as farfetched an idea in his time as it appears to many today. "Love your neighbor" and "Do unto others as you would have them do unto you" prescribe a simple yet comprehensive code of behavior. Thomas Jefferson, in the Declaration of Independence, reflected the values of many other thinkers of his era in declaring that all men are created equal; he thereby laid the groundwork for a great experiment in democracy. A modern-day ethicist, Mahatma Gandhi, championed the principle of achieving social and economic justice through nonviolent means. Common to Jesus, Jefferson, and Gandhi is a call to action based on a defined set of values.

The ethical foundation of public administration has been distorted by two perspectives, both of which amount to a refusal to acknowledge a defined set of values. One perspective is the model that divorces administration from policy making or from "politics"; the other is the effort to make political science more precise through empirical analysis and value-free behavioral studies. Emphasis on the "science" in political science coincided with the growing belief that it is wrong to "impose" value judgments—which has often come to mean that "it is wrong to make value judgments" or even that "it is wrong to acknowledge that you have values." This backing away from open discussion of values has impinged not only on public administration but on society in general.

James S. Bowman, in "Ethical Issues for the Public Manager," traces the abandonment of values to Woodrow Wilson, the father of the study of public administration. The distinction between policy making and policy execution was fundamental to Wilson's thinking, and the distinction was perpetuated by the supporters of the council-manager form of government. Bowman writes that this "dualism obscured ethical dimensions of public administration since it placed most administrators beyond the province of moral responsibility." In Bowman's view, confidence in the scientific method and concern about professional status combined to draw the profession and study of public administration away from concern with (or even acknowledgment of) values. With the abandonment of values came the "abdication of social responsibility."

Ralph Clark Chandler, in "The Problem of Moral Reasoning in Public Administration: The Case for a Code of Ethics," notes that

Weber also spoke of the "bureaucratic machine" in which the honor of the civil servant is vested in his or her ability to execute conscientiously the order of superior authorities, "exactly as if the order agreed with his own conviction." . . . Thus Weber's administrator considers it moral to avoid morality. . . . The organization schools itself in moral illiteracy.

Students of public administration are familiar with the Renaissance political philosopher who posited that the ruler of a state was not bound by common ethics. In *The Prince*, Machiavelli argues that the ends justify the means, that the prince must be prepared to lie, cheat, and be cruel to preserve order and protect his state.

Hans Reichenbach, in *The Rise of Scientific Philosophy*, argues forcefully that "the end logically requires the means." [2] In Reichenbach's view, it is a contradiction to believe that an end or a goal based on a certain set of values can or should be attained by a violation of those values.

The differentiation between "ends" (i.e., policies) and "means" (i.e., administration or policy execution) poses a dilemma for the public manager. After all, at the simplest level, public managers are only doing what they have been ordered to do. But what are the ethical considerations in honestly carrying out a dishonest policy? Can one morally pursue an immoral policy? These questions are variations on the old "ends-means" question, and the answer lies with Reichenbach: "The end logically requires the means."

In "Types and Levels of Public Morality," York Willbern frames the distinction well:

The ... distinction is that between consideration of the ethical behavior (honesty, rectitude) of the official and consideration of the moral content of the public policy or action the official promulgates or carries out. Most public criticism of public ethics focuses on the former; the concerns of the adherents of the "new public administration" were on the latter.

Willbern provides a framework within which to look at the public manager's responsibility—not only for his or her personal conduct but also for the content of the policies being administered.

In "The Possibility of Administrative Ethics," Dennis F. Thompson challenges the two viewpoints that leave the individual administrator free of responsibility for the policies of his or her organization. The first view, "the ethics of neutrality," holds that the administrator must follow the policies of the organization; the second, the "ethics of structure," holds that the organization as a whole is responsible for its decisions—not the individuals within the organization. In a powerful response to those who would argue about their degree of responsibility for any particular policy or decision, Thompson writes that "responsibility is not a bucket in which less remains when you apportion some out."

Ethics, as discussed in this book, is not about preaching or about guilt. Rather, it is about behavior. The purist would insist on a strict definition of "ethics," "values," and "morality," but ethics is an art, not a science. Reichenbach writes, "who looks for ethical rules must not imitate the methods of science. Science tells us what is, not what should be." [3] For discussion purposes, it is sufficient to say that *acting* according to a set of values produces an ethical system and that such an ethical system is judged to be moral (i.e., "good") to the extent that it improves society and the individuals who make up society.

Not rules but action is the dominant theme in this collection of articles. In "Ethical Managers Make Their Own Rules," Sir Adrian Cadbury points out that he is not talking about "pious righteousness" and that "our ethics are expressed in our actions, which is why they are usually clearer to others than to ourselves."

Some practitioners who read this book will be looking for practical guidelines or rules to help them fine tune their skills in ethical behavior in the public setting. However, the serious practitioner must approach ethics at a level deeper than that of personal behavior.

Effective public managers have never "just followed orders." Contrary to the folklore, effective public manangers do not draw a line between policy making and policy execution: they know that the two are inextricably intertwined. Effective public managers are not just gunslingers or hired hands who are expected to do a piece of work and then move on. To borrow a cliché from current management writing, the effective public manager must not only do things right; he or she must do the right thing.

Ralph Chandler, in "The Problem of Moral Reasoning in American Public Administration," presents the case for a code of ethics. The development of such guidelines, the clear statement of principles involved, the inculcation of these principles in an organization or a profession, and the enforcement of these principles are central to the goals of public administration. After all, as Bowman notes, "democratic governance relies heavily on personal integrity and trust and confidence between the public and its officials."

There is more to ethics, however, than codes of individual conduct. The International City Management Association has developed an adequate code of individual conduct in the ICMA Code of Ethics. A much more significant contribution is made by ICMA's "Declaration of Ideals," an unabashed expression of commitment to the values of democracy, citizen participation, individuality, equity, integration of cultures, responsiveness, excellence, opportunity, and personal growth.

Mark Pastin, in "The Thinking Manager's Toolbox," takes a practical approach to ethics as a tool to support organizational success. He warns, however, that "without a clear sense of your own ethics, you cannot develop a clear understanding of how to view your ethics in relation to the ethics of others and the organization." Developing that clear sense of your own ethics is often easier said than done. As Frank P. Sherwood writes in "Professional Ethics," "it is easy to underestimate the energy and effort required to face one's own value system and then to relate that to consciously personal decisions and behavior patterns."

Is it worth the effort? It *is* worth it to the responsible manager; as Pastin notes, "responsibility is the issue in almost every hard management problem, ethical or otherwise." Managers who must take responsibility both for their personal conduct and for the content of the policies they administer—no matter to what degree they participated in the formulation of those policies—must make the effort to develop a clear sense of their own ethics. Then, with the application of values such as are found in the ICMA Declaration of Ideals, the public manager can perhaps approach the vision of the public servant as described by Justice Louis Brandeis (quoted by Chandler):

They cannot be worthy of the respect and admiration of the people unless they add to the virture of obedience some other virtues—virtues of manliness, of truth, of courage, of willingness to risk criticism, of the willingness to risk the misunderstanding that so often comes when people do the heroic thing.

Reichenbach, the rational philosopher who recognized unreason, concludes his chapter on the nature of ethics as follows:

> Whenever there comes a philosopher who tells you that he has found the ultimate truth, do not trust him. If he tells you that he knows the ultimate good, or has a proof that the good must become reality, do not trust him, either. The man merely repeats the errors which his predecessors have committed for two thousand years. Ask the philosopher to be as modest as the scientist; then he may be as successful as the man of science. But do not ask him what you should do. Open your ears to your own will, and try to unite your will with that of others. There is no more purpose or meaning in the world than you put in it.[4]

Likewise, do not read these articles to determine what you should do. Read these articles to begin your exploration of your values and your determination of what is important to you as a public manager. The conscious identification of those values will provide the framework not only for your personal behavior but for your behavior in the public policy arena.

Notes

1. Mark Pastin, *The Hard Problems of Management: Gaining the Ethics Edge* (San Francisco: Jossey-Bass, 1986), 17.
2. Hans Reichenbach, *The Rise of Scientific Philosophy* (Berkeley: University of California Press, 1951), 279.
3. Ibid., 287.
4. Ibid., 302.

PART 1

The Individual in the Organization

Types and Levels of
Public Morality

York Willbern

Students of government and public administration, from Plato to Wilson and from Weber to the proponents of the "new public administration," have nearly always known that what public officials and employees do has a central and inescapable normative component, involving values, morality, and ethics,[1] although they may have differed as to the degree to which this component could be separated, either analytically or in practice, from aspects of administration involving facts, science, or technique. Discussions about moral considerations involving public officials, however, frequently deal with significantly different types of forces and phenomena.

The most obvious distinction is that between consideration of the ethical behavior (honesty, rectitude) of the official and consideration of the moral content of the public policy or action the official promulgates or carries out.[2] Most public criticism of public ethics focuses on the former; the concerns of adherents of the "new public administration" were on the latter.

Serious attention to the ethical and moral components of public officialdom suggests that there are other important distinctions also. This essay is primarily one of taxonomy; it attempts to identify and characterize particular components or facets of official ethics and morality in an effort to lay out a rough map of the terrain.[3] Classification is difficult in this area not only because of the overlapping of the concepts and the activities, but because of the ambiguities of the words used to describe them. Nevertheless, such an effort may be helpful in joining discussion and in making it more likely that people talk about comparable rather than different things.

While for some purposes it would be valuable to distinguish the ethical problems involving elected or politically appointed officials from those involving civil servants, or among those in particular aspects of public service (i.e., public works, social work, university teaching, or others), no concentrated attention will be given here to such differences.

It is suggested that six types, or levels, of morality for public officials can be discerned, with, perhaps, increasing degrees of complexity and subtlety. There are, of course, substantial interrelationships among these levels, but they are different enough to be analytically interesting. They are: (1) basic honesty and conformity to law; (2) conflicts of interest; (3) service orientation and procedural fairness; (4) the ethic of democratic responsibility; (5) the ethic of public policy determination; and (6) the ethic of compromise and social integration.

In general, the first two or lower levels (and in some degree the third) concern aspects of personal morality and and, hence, the ethical conduct of the individual public servant; the other, or higher, levels deal more with the morality of the governmental decisions or actions taken by the official or employee. Public scandals and outrage at unethical behavior focus mainly on the lower levels. Most public officials and employees are confronted with choices, as individuals, which involve ethical concerns at these levels. At the higher levels, most actions and decisions and policies in modern complex governments and bureaucracies are more collective, corporate, and institutional in nature, in which the individual moral responsibility is shared with others in complex ways. This is true even for chief executives; even if "the buck stops here," the bulk of the work in preparing "the buck" and its possible alternatives will have been done by others.

Basic honesty and conformity to law

The public servant is morally bound, just as are other persons, to tell the truth, to keep promises, to respect the person and property of others, and to abide by the requirements of the law. The law—the codes enacted or enforced by the legitimate organs of the state—usually embodies these basic obligations and provides sanctions for violating them. The law also includes many other requirements, and there is a moral obligation to conform, with arguable exceptions only in the most extreme circumstances. An orderly society cannot exist if individuals can choose to follow only those laws with which they agree; civil disobedience is an acceptable moral tactic only in very extreme situations. Conformity to law is especially necessary for public officials and employees.

These behaviors are basic requisites of an orderly society,

which exists only if people can be reasonably secure in their persons and belongings, can normally rely on the statements and commitments of others, and can expect others to conform to the established norms of conduct. There are, of course, liars and thieves and law breakers in the public sector, as there are in the private, and it is transgressors of this kind who are particularly noticeable and who bring public condemnation.

In general, the difficulties in interpreting and following these broad mandates are about the same for public servants as for others. Definitional problems (What is true, and should all the truth be told? What property belongs to whom? What is the law?) which produce moral dilemmas are probably no more difficult in the public sector than in the private.

Even at this level of basic honesty and conformity, however, there may be some ways in which the public service differs. To some observers, the fact that public officials are vested with the power of the state produces more danger and more opportunity for transgression of the basic moral code. Power and access to public goods may provide more temptation; the necessity to communicate and deal regularly with the public may lead to more occasion to prevaricate or to ignore promises and commitments.

This may be more true in other societies than in America. In this country, two factors seem to limit, in some degree, the relative danger of official misbehavior at this basic level. One is the obvious fact that power is less concentrated in the government. The power that is lodged in private economic institutions and aggregations, especially apparent in the United States, may be no less corrupting than the power of public officials. Ours is a rather pluralistic society, with countervailing powers scattered quite widely. A second and related factor is the existence of stronger and more independent control mechanisms in our system, especially stemming from the judiciary and the press. In the United States, every public official (even the president, as the last decade demonstrated) lives in the shadow of the courthouse. And in America, unlike many other systems, the same courts exercise control over public officials and private citizens. Moreover, the American press is particularly vigorous in trying to exercise surveillance over public officials and employees.

The visibility of public life may well make dishonest behavior less frequent there than in private life. Public officials are expected not to be honest, but to appear to be honest. Both Caesar and Caesar's wife are to be above reproach, and departures from that norm are noticed. There is almost certainly less tolerance of public employees than of private employees who deviate from accepted standards in such personal matters as marital behavior, sexual deviance, and the use of alcohol and drugs, as well as in basic honesty.

Some would argue that the nature of political discourse in a democratic system greatly increases the likelihood of falsehoods and insincere and broken promises. There is no doubt that political campaigns and even the prospect of such campaigns produce statements that are at least selective in their veracity, and that neither the makers nor the recipients of campaign promises seem too surprised if the promised performances do not fully materialize. Without questioning the immorality of campaign falsehoods and forgotten promises, the fact that knowledgeable listeners to puffery of this sort do not really take it too seriously nor depend upon it for their own decisions may mitigate somewhat the seriousness of the sin. The same sort of salt is applied to advertising and salesmanship assertions in the private marketplace; regulations such as those of the Federal Trade Commission and the Securities and Exchange Commission attempt, without complete success, to limit inaccurate allegations and promises. Campaign puffery aside, however, the importance of veracity and adherence to direct interpersonal political commitments is widely recognized.

There are, on the other hand, areas of public official behavior where deceit and lying are not only condoned but approved. The police use undercover agents and "sting" operations to try to catch criminals. Official falsehoods and deception certainly accompany foreign intelligence and some national defense activities. In covert operations in particular countries, public employees may go well beyond falsehood in contravening the normal moral code. These are very difficult ethical areas, where the end is presumed to justify the means, and *raison d'état* provides shaky moral justification.

Conflict of interest

The ethical problems associated with conflicts of interest in the public service are even more complex and difficult. The general presumption is that the moral duty of an official or employee of a unit of government is to pursue the "public interest"—i.e., the needs and welfare of the general body of citizens of the unit. His own interests, and the interests of partial publics of which he may be a member, are to be subordinated if they differ from the broader, more general, public interest—as they almost inevitably will, from time to time.

In their cruder manifestations, conflict of interest transgressions fit clearly into the category of ethical problems discussed above, the obligation to respect the property of others and to conform to the law. Embezzlement of public funds, bribery, and contract kickbacks are all actions in which the offenders have pursued their personal interests in obvious contravention of the public interest, as well as in violation of the law. Expense account padding is a more common illustration of both conflict of interest and of theft. There are generally laws against the more obvious conflicts of interest.

But there are also very difficult and subtle conflicts of interest that are not so clearly theft, and which may not involve law violation. At a simple level, to take a trip at public expense which may not have been necessary but which enabled the official to visit family or friends, or just to have a semi-vacation without using leave time, presents a problem of conflict of interest ethics, as does nepotism, or the appointment or advancement of a relative or friend—as is the case involving political party patronage systems.

Every public employee belongs to other groups than his governmental agency—church, professional, local community, racial, or ethnic group. Most officials and employees, especially those in public service for only limited periods, worked for and with someone else before the government, and may anticipate such employment after their government service. It is very easy to presume that the interests of those groups coincide with the interests of the entire public, but others may disagree. Moreover, officials have private financial investments which can be affected by public policy decisions.

Among the most difficult and subtle of the public service conflict of interest problems are those relating to the obvious and inevitable interest of a person or group or party to win elections. This is related to the ethic of democratic responsibility, to be discussed later. It is sufficient to note at this point that to award contracts or jobs or shape public policies in such a way as to reward people or groups for their past or expected campaign support rather than on the merits of the public purpose involved raises tough ethical questions.[4] Campaign financing, for example, may be one of the most vulnerable spots in a democratic system. Those who contribute to a successful campaign usually expect, and get, a degree of access to decision makers that raises questions about the even-handedness of decisions and actions.

There are conflicts of interest in private life, as well. In the private as in the public sector, people are imbedded in collective entities—corporations, firms, associations—and they are confronted with many occasions in which their personal or small group interests may conflict with those of the larger entity. The potential, and frequently real, conflicts of interest between the management and the stockholders of a corporation, or between management and rank-and-file employees, are obvious illustrations.

There is a very important difference between conflicts of interest in public life and in private life. A basic cornerstone of the Western economic system is that the vigorous pursuit of self-interest by each participant is the most effective way to secure the general interest—the "invisible hand" of the market will transform selfish pursuits into the general welfare. The presumption that what is good for General Motors is good for the country, and vice versa, seems a truism in the capitalist economic system. In spite of the variety of exceptions that modern economists will make, the power and pervasiveness of this idea make conflicts of interest in the private sector considerably different than in the public.

This vigorous pursuit of self-interest by private economic entities, in their relationships to government, is one of the great causes of moral problems in the public sphere. Modern government has great impact on economic activity, and every economic entity needs and wants to influence public policy in its own interest. Government can give and withhold privileges of great value. The tendency to presume that what is good for the particular group or social segment of which a person is a member is also good for others is almost irresistible.

Lincoln Steffens, in attempting to explain the cause of corruption in government, compared the situation to that in the Garden of Eden. The trouble, he said, was not the serpent—that was his nature. Nor was it the weakness of Eve, nor of Adam—they also did what was natural. The fault, he said, was in the apple.

It can be argued that the political world is also a marketplace, where the pursuit of self-interest by all the varying segments will produce a harmonious general welfare. This was essentially the argument of Madison in Federalist Paper number 10, suggesting that the enlargement of the polity would increase the number of interests participating in the political market, and thus make more likely the achievement of a general rather than a particular interest.

But governmental decision making is far more institutionalized that the decision making of a free economic market, and the public official is always torn between acting as proponent of an interest (his own, or that of his department or agency, or of his profession, or of his faction or party) and acting as an arbiter among competing interests. Should U.S. Senator Richard Lugar support the interests of Indiana coal miners in dealing with acid rain? Can a real estate developer serve impartially on a zoning board? A longtime public servant coined an aphorism that is now widely known in the public administration community as Miles' Law: "Where a man stands depends on where he sits."

Since both potential and real conflicts of interest are so pervasive, major efforts are made to provide a degree of protection by procedural safeguards (a subject to be considered further in connection with the next level of public morality). Public acknowledgement of outside interests is required, and arrangements are made for officials to refrain from participation in matters where their interests may conflict. But these safeguards are far from sufficient to remove the moral responsibility of the individual employee or officer.

Here, as in so many other moral matters, degree may become

crucial. Some conflict of interest is inevitable; the question becomes, how much conflict of interest taints a decision or action so much as to make it unethical?

Service orientation and procedural fairness

We now enter areas where the overlap with private morality, while still present, is less noticeable, and where the problems are more peculiarly those of public officials and employees.

The purpose of any governmental activity or program is to provide service to a clientele, a public. This is true even if the activity is in some degree authoritarian, a regulation or control. It is sometimes easy for this moral imperative to be obscured by the fact that government, and government officials, have and exercise power. The auditor at the Internal Revenue Service, the policeman on the beat, the teacher in the classroom, the personnel officer in an agency, are there to serve their clients, but they also exercise authority, and there is real moral danger in the possibility that the authority comes to overshadow the service.

Attitudes and the tone and flavor of official behavior are morally significant. Where power is being exercised, arrogance can easily replace humility, and the convenience of the official becomes more important than the convenience of the client. Delay and secrecy can become the norm. Procedures are designed for official purposes, not those of the public. This may well be the kind of corruption Lord Acton had in mind, rather than thievery or bribery, when he said that "power corrupts."

The effort to provide some degree of protection for the clients against the potential arrogance of officials is one of the reasons why procedural fairness is one of the central components of public morality. The concept that a person threatened with the power of the state has firm procedural rights is a very ancient one. The right to a trial, a public trial, or a hearing, with proper notice of what is alleged or intended, the right to counsel, the right of appeal, are built into administrative as well as judicial procedures. "Procedural due process" is a cornerstone of public morality.

In addition to the need to protect citizens against the corrupting power of the state officialdom, there is another important ground for a procedural component of public morality. As will be noticed further in connection with the sixth (highest?) level of morality to be discussed here, it is inevitable that in a complex society interests will be opposed to each other, that not all can be satisfied, and that often not even a Pareto optimality can be achieved. The public decision-making process may not be a zero-sum game, with inevitable losses accompanying all gains, but the difficulty of satisfying all makes it necessary that the *process* of arriving at decisions about action, or policy, be a fair one.

The ethic of democratic responsibility

In our consideration of various types and levels of public morality, another transition occurs. The first three levels deal with the conduct of public officials as they go about their business, the last three with the content of what they do. It is upon these first three levels (particularly the first two) that attention is usually focused in discussions of official ethics. They are important, and difficult, but they may not be as central as the considerations affecting the moral choices involved in deciding *what* to do, in pursuing the purposes of the state and the society. The first set might be said to deal with collateral morality, the latter set with intrinsic morality.

The dogma of the morality of popular sovereignty is now general throughout the world, and nowhere is it more strongly entrenched than in the United States. To be democratic is good, undemocratic bad. Observers acknowledge the existence of elites, even power elites, but the suggestion is that their presence is unfortunate and, by implication at least, immoral. Citizen participation is encouraged, even required, in governmental programs. Hierarchy is suspect, participatory management the goal, even within an agency or institution.

In spite of almost universal adherence to the dogma, there are some reservations about its practice. Government by referendum does not always arouse enthusiasm. "Maximum feasible participation"—the legal requirement for several national programs—was certainly not an unqualified success; U.S. Senator Patrick Moynihan called it "maximum feasible misunderstanding." Many have reservations about open records, open meetings, public negotiations—all justified on the grounds of the public's "right to know." But these reservations are still only "reservations"; the basic notion of popular sovereignty is seldom challenged.

In its simplest logic, the legitimacy of popular control is transmitted to operating public servants through a chain of delegation. The legislature is supposed to do what the people want, while the public executive and administrator are to conform to legislative intent. The politically chosen official, either elected or appointed by someone who was elected, has the mandate of the people. The civil servant is ethically bound to carry out the instructions of these politicians, who derive their legitimacy from the people. The military is subordinate to politically chosen civilians. The "career" officials or employees are supposed to carry out Republican policies during a Republican administration, Democratic policies during a Democratic administration, because that is what the people want. For public employees to substitute their own judgments as to what the people want for the judgment of those who have the electoral or political mandate is unethical, according to this logic. They may advise to the contrary, but they are to carry out the instructions of their political superiors to the best of their ability. If they cannot conscientiously do so, their only ethical choice is to resign their posts.

In reality, of course, the situation is never as clear as the simple logic suggests. In this country (more, probably, than in other practicing democracies), there are usually multiple rather than single channels for the expression of the public will. Both the legislature and the executive (sometimes many executives), and sometimes the judges, are elected by the people, and they may emit different signals from their popular mandates. A statute, or a constitutional provision, may be considered to embody the popular mandate better than instructions from a political superior. Arrangements for direct citizen participation through hearings or advisory commissions may complicate the process further. A public employee may have considerable range of choice in choosing which popular mandate to respond to. But, in principle, strong support would be given to the concept that a public official in a democracy has a moral responsibility to follow the will of the people in his or her actions.

This ethic of democratic responsibility, the logic of which is quite powerful, produces difficulty for public employees. The employees may have goals and values which differ from those transmitted through the political channels. Or, the political superiors, even the people themselves, may not be fully informed. There may be no better illustration than the resistance which professors in a public university might make to instructions from a board of trustees or a legislature as to what to teach or who should teach it.

The conflict is particularly severe when the logic of democracy conflicts with the logic of science or of professional expertise. What is the ethical position of the public employee when the people, directly or through their properly elected representatives, insist on the teaching of "creationism," which is repugnant to the scientist? Or when the certified experts say that fluoride in the water is good for people but the people say no? To put it in the simplest terms, should the public official give the people what they want or what he thinks they ought to want?

To some, the voice of the people in a democracy may be equivalent to the voice of God. But, for most public officials in most circumstances, that axiom will not provide answers that allow them to escape their personal responsibility to make moral choices based on their own values. The voice of the people will not be clear, it will not be based on full knowledge, it will conflict in small or large degree with other persuasive and powerful normative considerations.

Here, as in other situations, the most popular (perhaps the best) answer may be a relativistic one. The official may be responsive to democratic control and his political superiors, but not too much. Democracy may be interpreted not as government by the people, but as government with the consent of the people, with professionals (either in a functional field or as practicing political leaders) making most decisions on the basis of standards and values derived from sources other than a Gallup poll, and submitting to only an infrequent exercise of electoral judgment as to the general direction of policy. Civil servants carry out the instructions of their political superiors with vigor and alacrity if they agree with them, and with some foot-dragging and modification if they disagree. They try to give the people, and the political officials representing them, what they would want if they had full information, meaning of course, the information available to the person conducting the activity.

The ethic of public policy determination

Perhaps the most complex and difficult of all the moral levels is that involved in determining public policy, in making actual decisions about what to do. The problems of honesty and conformity to law, difficult as they sometimes are, are simple compared to those in decisions about public policy. And these are inescapably *moral* judgments; some policies, some actions, are good, some bad. Determinations about the nature of the social security program and how it is to be paid for, for example, turn only in minor degree on technical information; they depend chiefly on basic considerations about human values.

There can be no doubt that normative determinations are made at all levels of public service. They are not made just by legislatures, or by city councils, or school boards. They are also made by the street level bureaucrats—the policeman on the beat, the intake interviewer at the welfare office, the teacher in the classroom. These individuals make decisions in their official capacity that involve equity and justice and order and compassion. Rules, regulations, and supervision of others in a chain of command stretching back, in theory, to the sovereign people may provide a framework for decisions, but not a very tight framework. Every teacher knows that the department chairman and superintendent really have very little to do with how the job is actually done, and every cop knows the same thing about the police chief.

Though right and wrong certainly exist in public policy, they are frequently—usually—difficult to discern with confidence. There are degrees and levels of right and wrong. A medieval English verse about the enclosure of the village commons by the nobles goes:

The law locks up both man and woman
Who steals the goose from off the common,
But lets the greater felon loose
Who steals the common from the goose.[5]

The perpetrator of a regressive tax, or of a regulation which permits water or air used by thousands to be polluted, or of a foreign policy position which produces or enlarges armed conflict, may do far more harm to far more people than hundreds of common burglars. But is he or she a greater criminal? Or more immoral? The regressive tax may be better than leaving an essential public service unfunded; the pollution may result from a highway that allows people to go about their affairs expeditiously or from a power plant that permits them to air condition their homes; many reasonable people believe that the most effective way to deter armed conflict is to threaten, with serious intent, to initiate or escalate armed conflict.

The judgments that must be made about the rightness or wrongness of a public policy or decision involve at least two types of considerations—one, the benefit-cost calculation, and the other, the distributional problem (who gains and who loses).

Benefit-cost calculations are generally more difficult in the public arena than in the private, for two reasons. One is the matter of measurement—the currency in which the calculations are made. There are, of course, nonmonetary considerations in many private decisions, but they are more pervasive in public determinations. The other reason is the greater necessity for concern about externalities, for spillover costs and benefits. This is an important but usually secondary consideration in a private decision, but often central in a public one. The making of good benefit-cost calculations may be more a matter of wisdom (either analytical or intuitive) than of morality, but normative considerations in choosing factors to consider, and assigning weights to them, are inescapable.

Ethical considerations are particularly salient in determinations about *distribution* of benefits and burdens in a public activity or decision. Here we confront squarely the problems of equity and justice and fairness. Any attempt to define these concepts (which have occupied philosophers a long time) is obviously beyond the scope of this short paper. But a few reflections may be offered.

Policies which do not provide equal treatment for all, or which enhance rather than diminish inequality, are usually condemned as unjust and unfair. But equity is not synonymous with equality. Equity may require similar treatment for those who are similarly situated—but not all are similarly situated. Many public policies do, and should, discriminate. The critical question is whether the basis for differentiation and the kind of differentiation are appropriate. It is appropriate and desirable for public policy to reward desirable behavior and punish undesirable behavior. To give an A to one student and an F to another, and to admit one to graduate school and turn the other down, certainly discriminates, but it may be just and fair and equitable. A central purpose of social policy is to elicit desirable behavior, and discourage undesirable.

It is also usually considered appropriate on the basis of need—

to provide things for the widow and the orphan and the physically and mentally handicapped that are not provided for others. Compassion would certainly seem a morally defensible ground for such discrimination. And there are many other grounds for such discrimination, many of them morally debatable. For example, is it appropriate (ethical) to provide free education for a citizen but not for an alien? Is it ethical to deport a refugee from economic privation but not a refugee from political oppression? Is it inequitable, unjust, and unconstitutional to deviate from one-man–one-vote apportionment in electing members of state legislatures and city councils, but not in electing U.S. senators?

The ethic of compromise and social integration

To some, morality means uncompromising adherence to principle. To compromise with evil, or with injustice, is immoral. But "principle" and "evil" and "injustice" are not always certain, especially in complex social situations. One man's social justice may be another man's social injustice. Lincoln's classic formulation, "with firmness in the right as God gives us to see the right," seems to carry with it the implication that God may give someone else to see the right differently, and that he also may be firm.

We must live with each other, adjust to each other, and hence make compromises with each other. This is a central feature of politics and of a bureaucratic world that is also political. We are all involved in politics—the only place without politics was Robinson Crusoe's island before Friday came. As every successful politician knows, it is necessary upon occasion to rise above principle and make a deal. Thus, compromise can be viewed as a highly moral act—without concessions to those who disagree, disagreement becomes stalemate and then conflict.

If sincere people hold to differing values, there must be institutional arrangements which legitimize courses of action which certainly can not satisfy all and may not fully satisfy any, and there is a moral obligation for both citizens and officials, but particularly officials, to participate in and support such arrangements. These institutional arrangements are, in large degree, procedural, permitting and encouraging public policy discourse and mutual persuasion and, finally, resolution of differences. The needed public policy discourse is more than the discourse of a marketplace which involves bargaining between and among economic self-interests. It is somewhat different than the discourse in the "republic of science," in which evidence and proof (or at least disproof) can be marshalled. It may never attain the level of discourse which Habermas calls an "ideal speech situation." But it must be social discourse with a strongly moral component.

Since complete *substantive* due process, measured by the standards of a particular participant in the political process, can rarely be achieved, a large measure of *procedural* due process is a moral necessity, not only to protect an individual against the power of the state, but to make legitimate the process of public decision making. Complete reconciliation, or social integration, will always be elusive, but social cohesion, loyalty to and participation in a group, and in larger communities, is a moral goal of the highest order.

T.V. Smith put it this way: The world is full of saints, each of whom knows the way to salvation, and the role of the politician is that of the sinner who stands at the crossroad to keep saint from cutting the throat of saint. This may possibly be the highest ethical level of the public servant.

Notes

1. To the cynic, of course, the phrase Public Morality is an oxymoron—like Holy War, or United Nations, or Political Science.

2. This distinction has been pointed out by several writers—particularly by Wayne A.R. Leys in "Ethics and Administrative Discretion," *Public Administration Review 3* (Winter 1943), and in *Ethics for Policy Decisions* (New York: Prentice-Hall, 1952).

3. This outline map differs from others—and they differ from each other. Several which have been particularly suggestive, even though they differ, are the items by Leys cited in note 2, above; a particularly rich two-volume collection of papers edited by Harlan Cleveland and Harold Lasswell, *Ethics and Bigness* and *The Ethic of Power* (New York: Harper, 1962); two substantial essays by Edmond Cahn, *The Sense of Injustice* (Bloomington: Indiana University Press, 1964) and *The Moral Decision* (Bloomington: Indiana University Press, 1966); a volume by George A. Graham, *Morality in American Politics* (New York: Random House, 1952); and a lecture (unfortunately unpublished) given by Dwight Waldo at Indiana University in Bloomington in 1977.

4. A very sensitive description of such problems, based largely on his own experiences as mayor of Middletown, may be found in Stephen K. Bailey, "The Ethical Problems of an Elected Political Executive," in Cleveland and Lasswell (eds.), *Ethics and Bigness, op. cit.,* pp. 24–27.

5. I borrowed this from George Graham, *op. cit.,* p. 33. I'm sure he borrowed it from someone else.

The Moral Responsibility of Individuals in Public Sector Organizations

Debra W. Stewart

The concern about the need for more attention to questions of professional ethics is expressed regularly in the pages of journals addressing public administration.[1] Most recently it served as the catalyst for a public debate in the American Society for Public Administration over the appropriateness of a proposed code of ethics in public administration.[2] The debate, however, is not limited to managers in the public sector. In virtually all the major professions today there are lively discussions about how professionals cope with the ethical quandaries they face in their work lives. Lawyers, physicians, engineers, professors, even data processing professionals are publicly examining their collective consciences to discern the proper standards of conduct.[3]

In public administration much of this reflection focuses on developing or enhancing existing jurisdictional codes of ethics and conflict of interest statutes; some explore organizational protection for whistle-blowers; still other discussions consider enhancing the power of oversight committees and other monitoring groups to ensure that missteps will be exposed or discouraged. In these discussions across professions, one concern is common: to what extent should the individual be cast as a "moral actor" in a work setting? The extent to which this particular question dominates the debate about professional ethics correlates strongly with the extent to which the profession must be practiced as part of a collective. Where the sole professional is able to deliver a service to a client directly, issues of individual responsibility pale in comparison to issues of the morality of the interaction. Should a physician lie to a

Reprinted with permission from the Winter 1985 issue of *Public Administration Quarterly.*

dying patient about prospects for recovery? Should a lawyer maintain client confidentiality if it puts another person at risk? But in public sector organizations where large numbers of professionals are working through complex organizations to achieve broad public policy objectives, the traditional basis for "moral accountability," i.e., the relationship between the individual professional and his/her client, evaporates.[4] Hence, the first question for the public manager when faced with a moral quandary is often: "What right do I have to exercise moral judgment at all?"

Tentativeness around this question has a profoundly chilling effect on productive examination of personal moral responsibility. Such tentativeness is triggered by a perspective which sees morality as residing principally in the organization itself—its routines, its incentives, its constraints, and its opportunities. It follows that, if the organization itself is the moral agent, placing obligation on the individual is unrealistic and ultimately an inefficient strategy for enhancing the moral quality of organizational actions. To examine this proposition, it is important to clarify the meaning of individual moral obligation.

To say that people are morally responsible is to "[evaluate] their behavior relative to some principle or standard."[5] Evaluative responsibility doesn't imply legal responsibility. A morally responsible person may or may not be legally responsible. But moral responsibility does mean the ability to hold an individual blameworthy for an act carried out even though that act is carried out as part of a collective. The purpose of this article is to examine those arguments against placing moral responsibility with individual actors in public sector organizations.

Three formidable arguments are marshaled against assigning significant moral responsibility to individuals in organizations: the argument from role, the argument from systems theory, and the argument from executive accountability. Each of these arguments will be presented and assessed with the objective of bringing sufficient closure to the question to permit further development in the management ethics field.

The argument from role

Roles are sets of sanctioned, expected behaviors in an organizational setting.[6] The argument from role suggests that, when one acts in an organizational role, "pursuing objectives and employing methods designated by it," one doesn't satisfy the necessary conditions for being held morally responsible. An individual can be morally responsible for actions only if "the action is free and the individual is himself at the time of the action."[7] Individuals bound by organizational roles are not free in this sense. This absence of freedom stems from the fact that they are acting as the representative of the organization and, as such, are obligated to carry through on past commitments and decisions as well as those dictated by their current roles. They are acting in a public rather than a private capacity. Acts taken by individuals in organizational roles as distinct from private roles are, in other words, acts taken by individuals within roles they themselves did not define.[8] Hence, conditions of moral responsibility cannot be met, not even in the sense of apportioning to individuals part of the collective responsibility of the group.

The counter-argument here can be summarized in four points. The first three points address role-governed behavior in any organization and the fourth point focuses on special characteristics of the public administration role. First, unless one is coerced to play a role, the fact that behavior is role governed doesn't relieve one of the moral responsibility for actions and their consequences. While some work organizations might provide more opportunity for individuals to change, rather than escape from, an objectionable state of affairs, no organization compels individuals to stay. In A. O. Hirschman's terms, both "Exit" and "Voice" remain viable options.[9] Admittedly, the lack of another organization in which to practice one's profession might hold exit at bay. But the nature of modern work organizations is that the prohibition of the exit option doesn't exist.

Second, the distinction between public and private acts which relieve individuals of responsibility for acts undertaken in their public role fails because individuals generally gain some personal benefit from performance of their public or organizational role. While advancing organization objectives, personal goals are also served—at the minimum by compensation for time and effort. In other words, the role is one means of securing personal ends.[10]

The third point is that, notwithstanding constraints implied by roles, individuals bring their own moral qualities to any position. All that is required for behavior is never totally spelled out by a role definition. Even role-constrained decisions permit individual judgments, reflecting the unique moral make-up of the decision-maker.[11]

All of the counter-arguments presented thus far portray a scenario where there is tension between the demands of a morally neutral role and individual judgments of right or wrong. However, this discussion of moral judgment in public sector organizational roles introduces a new factor because the very setting of the role implies a moral dimension. The historic debate in public administration over the proper mix of politics and administration highlights the central place of values in interpreting the public administrator's role. One might attribute this emphasis to historical circumstances, since the founders of our field were deeply involved with political reform movements before, during, and after the progressive era.[12] Or the source of the moral emphasis in the public administrator's role may simply be in the nature of the work to be done. Ralph Chandler notes, "Most public policy has as its declared aim some public good," and Dwight Waldo has identified more than a dozen sources of obligation relevant to the conduct of the public administrator's role.[13] Whatever the reason, the role of a public administrator carries a kind of moral weight not found in private sector counterpart roles.

The argument from systems theory

The second argument against assigning significant moral responsibility to individuals in organizations relates to the nature of complex organizations. Complex organizations are systems composed of several components which interact with one another to create a whole. Component parts include people, processes, structures, and cultures. Organizations have boundaries which differentiate them from their environment, but they interact with their environment regularly. Organizations, driven by systemic imperatives, convert inputs from the environment into outputs impacting the environment. Organizations are constantly interacting with the environment, changing and adapting to develop congruence between people, processes, structures, and sectors in the external environment.[14]

Thus, behavior in the organization can be understood less as the deliberate choice of specific people and more as "outputs" of large systems functioning according to standard patterns of behavior.[15] In order for large organizations to function, the behavior of large numbers of individuals must be coordinated. Coordination is achieved through organizational routines—a fixed set of standard operating procedures. "The behavior of these organizations . . . relevant to an issue in any particular instance is determined primarily by routines established in that organization prior to a particular event."[16] These routines change incrementally in response to changes in the environment.

The diverse demands on individuals shape their priorities, perceptions, and issues, but these demands emanate from position in the organization and the degree and character of interaction with sectors in the environment. Assigning responsibility for "moral reasoning" to individuals in this net of organizational system forces is inappropriate. Certainly, conflicts will arise between individuals and groups within organizations as they pursue their goals along the rails of established routines. But to cast these systemic conflicts as ethical dilemmas for the participant is an error.[17]

The counter-argument to the systems analysis rationale against holding individuals accountable has two parts. First, the systems approach to analyzing organizations is a descriptive and not a prescriptive enterprise. Systems theory is advanced to help us understand how organizations *do* behave, not how individuals *should* behave. For example, a major insight from systems theory as applied to organizations is that organizations, like all systems, are impelled toward survival and will adapt toward that objective. While survival makes perfect sense as a goal (i.e., we can better understand organizations by seeing them as systems striving to survive), survival is not the right objective in every situation. Some organizations should cease functioning from a public interest viewpoint. Any argument that individuals can't be held accountable because they are just part of the organizational system makes the error of confusing "system" as a description with "system" as a prescription. System is a metaphor to describe how organizations function; it can't be used to address the question of normative judgment in organizations.

Second, even as a metaphor of organizational life, systems theory is deficient when it ignores the political process that unfolds in an organization. Organizational power holders in "dominant coalitions" decide on courses of strategic action which both establish structural forms and manipulate environmental factors. In doing so, these collections of individuals make significant value choices which advance some goals and inhibit others. Thus, even in a descriptive sense, the dominant coalition in an organization is not at the mercy of the organization as a system.[18] Significant "outputs" are intentional. In deciding on courses of action, individuals are engaging in behavior that will help or hurt specific interests. For their contribution to such action, they are individually accountable.

The argument from executive accountability

The third argument against assigning moral responsibility to organizational members is that it places emphasis on "good people" rather than on executive accountability where it belongs. The ultimate objective of the focus on management ethics is to reduce unethical behavior in organizations. In reality, unethical behavior is reduced only by strategies which place individuals in fewer compromising situations (rotation, clear guidelines, etc.) and by increasing sanctions for illegal action.[19] Since the objective is actually to change the unethical behavior, that is where the focus should remain. To ensure that strategies for reducing opportunities for unethical action are adopted, responsibility should be placed at the top of the organization, in the office of the CEO.

The response to this assertion is not so much that the analysis is wrong; it is not. Whatever steps can be taken to buffer public servants from "occasions of sin" should be taken. Efforts to induce CEOs to adopt preventative measures to ensure that their subordinates avoid unethical action are worth considering. That is particularly so where the focus is on unethical actions which constitute a violation of the law.

However, at some level we also want to "get better people." The moral quality of our public servants is important because the alternative approach, if relied on exclusively, means to tighten control in a way that makes the exercise of moral judgment on the part of individuals unnecessary or impossible. We know that "the capacity to make moral judgment is strengthened by enabling members of organizations to respond to situations, to project alternative ends-in-view to solve those problems, devise means to reach ends and test their self-generated moral judgments in use."[20] The experience in lack of opportunity to make moral judgments increases the moral degeneration of organizational life. In other words, it might be advisable to put substantial energy into reducing the occasions of sin for public administrators, particularly in those areas where sin translates into violation of civil and criminal law. But this strategy, if used exclusively, will produce the undesirable consequence of a trained incapacity for moral judgment in the large majority of public managers not occupying CEO slots.

Conclusion

Is it appropriate to consider the public administrator an ethical agent in his or her work setting? In this author's opinion, the answer is "yes." The preceding analysis of arguments to the contrary compels the conclusion that public administrators find no easy escape from the uncomfortable task of making moral judgments. Inevitably moral quandaries arise because not all claimants can be equally served, not all goods are equally compatible, and not all outcomes are equally desirable. There is no simple moral equation which political executives use to generate the "right" solution to moral quandaries. In their work lives, public administrators will be confronted by choices weighted with ethical implications.

Helping to develop the "art of voice" is part of the task of public administration scholars.[21] The first step is to clear the decks with respect to the question of exercising moral judgment at all. This article is an attempt to achieve that goal.

Notes

1. A recent computer search on the Public Affairs Information Service data base revealed that the term *ethics* (or some variation, such as *ethical*) appeared in the title of publications covered on an average of 39 times a year from 1977 to 1982. As a percentage of total citations in the PAIS data base, the number of ethics citations has grown gradually since 1981, with the percentage doubling from 1982 to 1983.
2. The Professional Standards and Ethics Committee of the American

Society for Public Administration debated whether a code of ethics should be adopted for ASPA. In late 1981, after much heated discussion, the National Council of ASPA decided to adopt a statement of principles in lieu of a code of ethics. [In 1984, ASPA's National Council did adopt a Code of Ethics; implementation guidelines were adopted in 1985.]
3. Many examples would illustrate these discussions in the various professional fields. For representative

discussions in each field, see the following: Monroe H. Freeman, *Lawyers' Ethics in an Adversary System* (Indianapolis and New York: Bobbs-Merrill Co., 1975); S. J. Reiser, A. J. Dyck, and W. J. Curran, eds., *Ethics in Medicine* (Cambridge and London: MIT press, 1977); Rachelle Hollander, "Conference Report: Engineering Ethics," *Science, Technology, and Human Values* (Winter 1983); George M. Schorr, "Toward a Code of Ethics for Academics," *Journal of Higher Education* 53, no. 3 (1983); "DPMA Puts Bite in New Professional Ethics Code," *Information Systems News*, 7.

4. Robert A. Anderson, Robert Perrucci, Dan E. Schendel, and Leon E. Trachtmase, *Divided Loyalties: Whistle-Blowing at BART* (West Lafayette, IN: Purdue University, 1980).

5. Albert Flores and Deborah C. Johnson, "Collective Responsibility and Professional Roles," *Ethics* 93 (April 1983): 538.

6. Debra W. Stewart and G. David Garson, *Organizational Behavior and Public Management* (New York: Marcel Dekker, 1983).

7. Flores and Johnson, "Collective Responsibility," 541.

8. Ibid.

9. Albert O. Hirschman, *Exit, Voice, and Loyalty* (Cambridge: Harvard University Press, 1970).

10. Flores and Johnson, "Collective Responsibility."

11. Ibid.

12. Dwight Waldo, *The Enterprise of Public Administration* (Novato, CA: Chandler and Sharp, 1980), 93.

13. Ralph Clark Chandler, "The Problem of Moral Reasoning in American Public Administration: The Case for a Code of Ethics," *Public Administration Review* 43 (January/February 1983): 37; Waldo, *Enterprise of Public Administration*, 110.

14. Daniel Katz and Robert L. Kahn, *The Social Psychology of Organizations* (New York: John Wiley and Sons, 1966).

15. Graham T. Allison, *The Essence of Decision* (Boston: Little, Brown, 1971).

16. Ibid., 68.

17. The recent case study of whistle-blowing at the Bay Area Rapid Transit (BART) makes this case forcefully; see Anderson et al., *Divided Loyalties.*

18. John Child, "Organizational Structure, Environment and Performance: The Role of Strategy Choice," *Sociology* 6 (January 1972): 1-23.

19. Jameson W. Doig, "Placing the Burden Where It Belongs: The Role of Senior Executives in Preventing Illegal Behavior in Complex Organizations" (Paper prepared for the panel on "Anti-Corruption Strategies in Public Agencies" at the National Conference of the American Society for Public Administration, New York, April 16-19. Readers should note that Professor Doig's stress in advocating executive accountability is in reducing illegal behavior. This article considers behavior that may be perceived as unethical, though not necessarily illegal.

20. Larry D. Spence, "Moral Judgment and Bureaucracy," in Richard W. Wilson and Gordon J. Schochet, eds., *Moral Development and Politics* (New York: Praeger, 1980), 146.

21. Hirschman, *Exit, Voice, and Loyalty*, 43.

The Possibility of
Administrative Ethics

Dennis F. Thompson

Is administrative ethics possible? The most serious objections to administrative ethics arise from two common conceptions of the role of individuals in organizations—what may be called the ethic of neutrality and the ethic of structure. Both of these views must be rejected if administrative ethics is to be possible.

Administrative ethics involves the application of moral principles to the conduct of officials in organizations.[1] In the form with which we are primarily concerned here (ethics in public organizations), administrative ethics is a species of political ethics, which applies moral principles to political life more generally. Broadly speaking, moral principles specify (a) the rights and duties that individuals should respect when they act in ways that seriously affect the well-being of other individuals and society; and (b) the conditions that collective practices and policies should satisfy when they similarly affect the well-being of individuals and society. Moral principles require a disinterested perspective. Instead of asking how an action or policy serves the interest of some particular individual or group, morality asks whether the action or policy serves everyone's interest, or whether it could be accepted by anyone who did not know his or her particular circumstances, such as race, social class, or nationality. Moral judgments presuppose the possibility of a person to make the judgment and a person or group of persons to be judged.

The most general challenge to administrative ethics would be to deny the possibility of ethics at all or the possibility of political ethics. Although a worthy challenge, it should not be the primary concern of defenders of administrative ethics. Theorists (as well as practitioners when they think about ethics at all) have been so preoccupied with general objections to ethics that they have neglected objections that apply specifically to ethics in administration. They have not sufficiently considered that even if we accept the possibility of morality in general and even in politics, we may have doubts it in organizations.

To isolate more specifically the objections to administrative ethics, we should assume that the moral perspective can be vindicated and that some moral principles and some judgments are valid. Despite disagreement about how morality is to be justified and disagreement about its scope and content, we nevertheless share certain attitudes and beliefs to which we can appeal in criticizing or defending public actions and policies from a moral perspective.[2]

The more direct challenge to administrative ethics comes from those who admit that morality is perfectly possible in private life but deny that it is possible in organizational life. The challenge is that by its very nature administration precludes the exercise of moral judgment. It consists of two basic objections—the first calls into question the subject of the judgment (who may judge); the second, the object of judgment (who is judged). The first asserts that administrators ought to act neutrally in the sense that they should follow not their own moral principles but the decisions and policies of the organization. This is the ethic of neutrality. The second asserts that not administrators but the organization (and its formal officers) should be held responsible for its decisions and policies. This is the ethic of structure. Each is called an ethic because it expresses certain norms and prescribes conduct. But neither constitutes an ethic or a morality because each denies one of the presuppositions of moral judgment—either a person to judge or a person to be judged.

The ethic of neutrality

The conventional theory and practice of administrative ethics holds that administrators should carry out the orders of their superiors and the policies of the agency and the government they serve.[3] On this view, administrators are ethically neutral in the sense that they do not exercise independent moral judgment. They are not expected to act on any moral principles of their own, but are to give effect to whatever principles are reflected in the orders and policies they are charged with implementing. They serve the organization so that the organization may serve society. Officials are morally obliged to serve the organization in this way because their acceptance of office is voluntary: it signifies consent. Officials know in advance what the duties of office will be, and if the duties (or their minds) change, officials can usually leave office.

The ethic of neutrality does not deny that administrators often must use their own judgment in the formulation of policy. But their aim should always be to discover what policy other people (usually elected officials) intend or would intend; or, in the case of conflicting directives, to interpret legally or constitutionally who has the authority to determine policy. The use of discretion on this view can never be the occasion for applying any moral principles other than those implicit in the orders and policies of the superiors to whom one is responsible in the organization. The ethic of neutrality portrays the ideal administrator as a completely reliable instrument of the goals of their organization, never injecting personal values into the process of furthering these goals. The ethic thus reinforces the great virtue of organization—its capacity to serve any social end irrespective of the ends that individuals within it favor.

A variation of the ethic of neutrality gives some scope for individual moral judgment until the decision or policy is "final." On this view, administrators may put forward their own views, argue with their superiors, and contest proposals in the process of formulating policy. But once the decision or policy is final, all administrators fall into line, and faithfully carry out the policy. Furthermore, the disagreement must take place within the agency and according to the agency's rules of procedure. This variation puts neutrality in abeyance, but "suspended neutrality" is still neutrality, and the choice for the administrator remains to "obey or resign." [4]

Three sets of criticisms may be bought against the ethic of neutrality. First, because the ethic underestimates the discretion that administrators exercise, it impedes the accountability of administrators to citizens. The discretion of administrators goes beyond carrying out the intentions of legislators or the superiors in the organization, not only because often there are no intentions to discover, but also because often administrators can and should take the initiative in proposing policies and mobilizing support for them. [5] The ethic of neutrality provides no guidance for this wide range of substantive moral decision making in which administrators regularly engage. By reinforcing the illusion that administrators do not exercise independent moral judgment, it insulates them from external accountability for the consequences of many of their decisions.

A second set of objections centers on the claim that officeholding implies consent to the duties of office as defined by the organization. While it may be easier to resign from office than from citizenship, it is for many officials so difficult that failure to do so cannot be taken to indicate approval of everything the organization undertakes. For the vast majority of governmental employees, vested rights (such as pensions and seniority) and job skills (often not transferable to the private sector) supply powerful incentives to hold on to their positions. Even if on their own many would be prepared to sacrifice their careers for the sake of principle, they cannot ignore their responsibilities to their families. Higher level officials usually enjoy advantages that make resignation a more feasible option. They can return to (usually more lucrative) positions in business or in a profession. But their ability to do so may depend on their serving loyally while in government, demonstrating that they are the good "team players" on whom any organization, public or private, can rely.

Furthermore, the dynamics of collective decision making discourage even conscientious officials from resigning on principle. Many decisions are incremental, their objectionable character apparent only in their cumulative effect. An official who is involved in the early stages of escalations of this kind (such as aid increases, budgets cuts, troop commitments) will find it difficult to object to any subsequent step. The difference between one step and the next is relatively trivial, certainly not a reason to resign on principle. Besides, many decisions and policies represent compromises, and any would-be dissenter can easily be persuaded that because his opponents did not get everything they sought, he should settle for less than what his principles demand. For these and other reasons, an official may stay in office while objecting to the policies of government; a failure to resign therefore does not signify consent.

Proponents of the ethic of neutrality may still insist that officials who cannot fulfill the duties of their office must resign, however difficult it may be to do so. But as citizens we should hesitate before endorsing this as a general principle of administrative ethics. If this view were consistently put into practice, public offices would soon be populated only by those who never had any reason to disagree with anything the government decided to do. Men and women of strong moral conviction would resign rather than continue in office, and we would lose the services of the persons who could contribute most to public life.

Because we do not want to drive persons of principle from office, we should recognize that there may be good moral reasons for staying in office even while disagreeing with the policies of the government. This recognition points to a third set of objections to the ethic of neutrality—that it simplifies the moral circumstances of public office. It tends to portray officials as assessing the fit between their moral principles and the policies of the organization, obeying if the principles and policies match, resigning if they diverge too much. What is important on this view is that in resigning, the individual express "ethical autonomy," which Weisband and Franck, in their otherwise valuable plea for resignations in protest, define as "the willingness to assert one's own principled judgment, even if that entails violating rules, values, or perceptions of the organization, peer group or team." [6] "The social importance of ethical autonomy," they write, "lies not in what is asserted but in the act of asserting." The ethic of neutrality encourages this and similar portrayals of an isolated official affirming his of her own principles against the organization at the moment of resignation. The ethic thereby neglects important considerations that an ethical administrator should take into account in fulfilling the duties while in office.

First of all, as an official you have obligations to colleagues, an agency, and the government as a whole. By accepting office and undertaking collective tasks in an organization, you give others reason to rely on your continued cooperation. Your colleagues begin projects, take risks, and make commitments in the expectation that you will continue to play your part in the organization. If you resign, you disappoint these expectations, and in effect break your commitments to your colleagues. A resignation may disrupt many organizational activities, some of which may be morally more important than the policy that occasions the resignation. An official must consider his commitments to all of his associates in government and the effect of his intended resignation on the conduct of government as a whole. Officials also have more general obligations to the public. Officials should not decide simply whether they can in good conscience continue to associate themselves with the organization. This could be interpreted as merely wanting to keep one's own hand clean—a form of what some have called "moral self-indulgence." [7]

A third way in which the ethic of neutrality distorts the duties of public administrators is by limiting their courses of action to two—obedience or resignation. Many forms of dissent may be compatible with remaining in office, ranging from quiet protest to illegal obstruction. Some of these, of course, may be morally wrong except under extreme circumstances, but the ethic of neutrality provides no guidance at all here because it rules out, in advance, the possibility of morally acceptable internal opposition to decisions of the organization, at least "final decisions."

The problem, however, is how we can grant officials scope for dissent without undermining the capacity of the organization to accomplish its goals. If the organization is pursuing goals set by a democratic public, individual dissent in the organization may subvert the democratic process. We should insist, first of all, that would-be dissenters consider carefully the basis of their disagreement with the policy in question. Is the disagreement moral or merely political? This is a slippery distinction since almost all important political decisions have moral dimensions. But perhaps we could say that the more directly a policy seems to violate an important moral principle (such as not harming innocent persons), the more justifiable dissent becomes. An official would be warranted in stronger measures of opposition against decisions to bomb civilian targets in a guerilla war than against decisions to lower trade barriers and import duties.[8] In cases of political disagreement of the latter sort, straightforward resignation seems the most appropriate action (once the decision is final). Dissenters must also consider whether the policy they oppose is a one-time incident or part of a continuing pattern and whether the wrongness of the policy is outweighed by the value of the other policies the organization is pursuing. Furthermore, dissenters must examine the extent of their own involvement and role: how (formally and informally) responsible are they for the policy? What difference would their opposition make to the policy and to the other policies of the organization? To what extent does the policy violate the ethics of groups to which they are obligated (such as the canons of the legal or medical professions)?

These considerations not only determine whether an official is justified in opposing the organization's policy, but they also help to indicate what methods of dissent the official may be justified in using to express opposition. The more an official's opposition, the more justified the official is in using more extreme methods. The methods of dissent may be arrayed on a continuum from the most extreme to the most moderate. Four types of dissent will illustrate the range of this continuum and raise some further issues that any would-be dissenter must consider.

First, there are those forms of dissent in which an official protests within the organization but still helps implement the policy, or (a slightly stronger measure) asks for a different assignment in the organization. In its weakest form, this kind of dissent does not go much beyond the ethic of neutrality. But unlike that ethic, it would permit officials to abstain from active participation in a policy they oppose and to continue their protest as long as they do so in accordance with the accepted procedures of the organization.[9]

One danger of this form of protest is what has been called the "domestication of dissenters." [10] A case in point is George Ball, who as undersecretary of state in the Johnson administration persistently argued against the government's Vietnam policy in private meetings:

Once Mr. Ball began to express doubts, he was warmly institutionalized: he was encouraged to become the in-house devil's advocate on Vietnam. ... The process of escalation allowed for periodic requests to Mr. Ball to speak his piece; Ball felt good ... (he had fought for righteousness); the others felt good (they had given a full hearing to the dovish option); and there was a minimal unpleasantness.[11]

In this way dissenters can be "effectively neutralized," and contrary to their intentions, their dissent can even help support the policy they oppose. It is important therefore to consider whether this effect is inevitable, and, if not, to discover the conditions under which it can be avoided.

In a second form of dissent, officials, with the knowledge of, but against the wishes of their superiors, carry their protest outside the organization while otherwise performing their jobs satisfactorily. This is the course of action taken by most of the 65 Justice Department attorneys who protested the decision to permit delays in implementing desegregation decrees in Mississippi in August of 1969.[12] The attorneys signed and publicized a petition denouncing the Attorney-General and the President for adopting a policy the attorneys believed violated the law and would require them to act contrary to the ethical canons of the legal profession. They also believed that resignation would not fulfill their obligation to act affirmatively to oppose illegality. Several of the dissenters argued for stronger actions that would directly block the policy, and some gave information to the NAACP Legal Defense Fund, which was opposing the Justice Department in court. Most of the attorneys declined to engage in these stronger actions, however, on the grounds that obstruction would weaken public support for their dissent.

This kind of dissent usually depends, for its efficacy as well as its legitimacy, on the existence of some widely accepted standards to which the dissenters can appeal outside the organization. Professional ethics or even the law may not be sufficient, since people disagree on how to interpret both, but appealing to such standards may at least reassure the public that the dissenters are not using their office to impose the dictates of their private consciences on public policy. When dissenters oppose democratically elected officials, they must find ways to show that they are defending principles that all citizens would endorse.

The third form of dissent is the open obstruction of policy. Officials may, for example, withhold knowledge or expertise that the organization needs to pursue the policy, refuse to step aside so that others can pursue it, or give information and other kinds of assistance to outsiders who are trying to overturn the policy. A few officials may adopt this strategy for a short time, but organizations can usually isolate the dissenters, find other officials to do the job, and mobilize its own external support to counter any opposition that arises outside the organization. In any such event, the dissenters are not likely to retain much influence within the organization. Effective and sustained opposition has to be more circumspect.

We are therefore led to a fourth kind of dissent: covert obstruction. Unauthorized disclosure—the leak—is the most prominent example. Leaks vary greatly in purpose and effect. Some simply provide information to other agencies that are entitled to receive it; others embarrass particular officials within an agency but do not otherwise subvert the agency's policies; others release information to the press or public, ultimately reversing a major government policy; and at the extreme, still others give secrets to enemy agents and count as treason. Short of that extreme, we still may want to say that unauthorized disclosure is sometimes justified even when it breaches government procedures or violates the law, as in the release of classified documents.

An analogy is sometimes drawn between official disobedience and civil disobedience. Many democratic theorists hold that citizens in a democracy are justified in breaking the law with the aim of changing a law or policy, but only in certain ways and under certain conditions. Citizens must (1) act publicly; (2) commit no violence; (3) appeal to principles shared by other citizens; (4) direct their challenge against a substantial injustice; (5) exhaust all normal channels of protest before breaking a law; and (6) plan their disobedience so that it does not, in conjunction with that of other citizens, disrupt the stability of the democratic process.[13]

Even if one thinks that civil disobedience is justifiable, one may not agree that official disobedience is warranted. Officials cannot claim the same rights as citizens can, and, it may be said, the analogy does not in general hold. But the analogy may not hold for the opposite reason. In extreme cases of governmental wrongdoing, so much is at stake that we should give officials greater scope for disobedience than we allow citizens. In these cases we might be prepared to argue that the standard conditions for civil disobedience are too restrictive for officials. If we insist, for example, that disobedience always be carried out in public, we may in effect suppress much valuable criticism of government. Fearful of the consequences of public action, dissenting officials may decide against providing information that their superiors have declared secret but that citizens ought to know. The point of relaxing the requirement of publicity would be not to protect the rights of dissenters for their sake but to promote public discussion of questionable actions of government. We may wish to retain some form of the requirement of publicity, perhaps by establishing an authority to whom a dissenter must make his or her identity known. But this requirement, as well as the others, should be formulated with the goal of maximizing the responsibility of governmental officials, not with the aim of matching exactly the traditional criteria of civil disobedience.

The important task, with respect to disobedience as well as the other forms of dissent, is to develop the criteria that could help determine when each is justifiable in various circumstances. The ethic of neutrality makes that task unnecessary by denying that ethics is possible in administration. But, as we have seen, that administrative neutrality itself is neither possible nor desirable.

The ethic of structure

The second major obstacle to administrative ethics is the view that the object of moral judgment must be the organization or the government as a whole. This ethic of structure asserts that, even if administrators may have some scope for independent moral judgment, they cannot be held morally responsible for most of the decisions and policies of government. Their personal moral responsibility extends only to the specific duties of their own office for which they are legally liable.

Moral judgment presupposes moral agency. To praise or blame someone for an outcome, we must assume that the person is morally responsible for the action. We must assume (1) that the person's actions or omissions were a cause of the outcome; and (2) that the person did not act in excusable ignorance or under compulsion. In everyday life, we sometimes withhold moral criticism because we think a person does not satisfy one or both of these criteria. But since usually so few agents are involved and because the parts they play are obvious enough, we are not normally perplexed about whether anyone can be said to have brought about a particular outcome. The main moral problem is what was the right thing to do, not so much who did it. In public life, especially organizations, the problem of identifying the moral agents, of finding the persons who are morally responsible for a decision or policy, becomes at least as difficult as the problem of assessing the morality of the decision or policy. Even if we have perfect information about all the agents in the organizational process that produced an outcome, we may still be puzzled about how to ascribe responsibility for it. Because many people contribute in many different ways to the decisions and policies of an organization, we may not be able to determine, even in principle, who is morally responsible for those decisions and policies. This has been called "the problem of many hands,"[14] and the assumption that it is not solvable underlies the ethic of structure.

Proponents of the ethic of structure put forward three arguments to deny the possibility of ascribing individual responsibility in organizations and thereby to undermine the possibility of administrative ethics. First, it is argued that no individual is a necessary or sufficient cause of any organizational outcome.[15] The contributions of each official are like the strands in a rope. Together they pull the load: no single strand could do the job alone, but the job could be done without any single strand. Suppose that for many decades the CIA has had a policy of trying to overthrow Third World governments that refuse to cooperate with their operatives, and suppose further that many of these attempts are morally wrong. No one presently in the agency initiated the practice, let us assume, and no one individual plays a very important role in any of the attempts. If any one agent did not do his or her part, the practice would continue, and even particular attempts would still often succeed. How could we say that any individual is the cause of this practice?

A second argument points to the gap between individual intention and collective outcomes. The motives of individual officials are inevitably diverse (to serve the nation, to help citizens, to acquire power, to win a promotion, to ruin a rival). Many praiseworthy policies are promoted for morally dubious reasons, and many pernicious policies are furthered with the best of intentions. In many organizations today, for example, we may well be able to say that no official intends to discriminate against minorities in the hiring and promoting of employees; yet the pattern of appointments and advancements still disadvantages certain minorities. Here we should want to condemn the pattern or policy (so the argument goes), but we could not morally blame any individual official for it.

A third argument stresses the requirements of role. The duties of office and the routine of large organizations require individual actions which, in themselves harmless or even in some sense obligatory, combine to produce harmful decisions and policies by the organization. Although the policy of the organization is morally wrong, each individual has done his or her moral duty according to the requirements of office. The collective sum is worse than its parts. In a review of the policies that led to financial collapse of New York City in the mid-1970s and endangered the welfare and livelihoods of millions of citizens, one writer concludes that no individuals can be blamed for the misleading budgetary practices that helped bring about the collapse: "The delicately balanced financial superstructure was a kind of evolutionary extrusion that had emerged from hundreds of piecemeal decisions." [16]

If we were to accept these arguments, we would let many guilty officials off the moral hook. Without some sense of personal responsibility, officials may act with less moral care, and citizens may challenge officials with less moral effect. Democratic accountability is likely to erode. How can these arguments be answered so that individual responsibility can be maintained in organizations?

First, we should not assess an official's moral responsibility solely according to the proportionate share he or she contributes to the outcome. "Responsibility is not a bucket in which less remains when some is apportioned out." [17] If a gang of 10 thugs beats an old man to death, we do not punish each thug for only one-tenth of the murder (even if no single thug hit him hard enough to cause his death). Further, in imputing responsibility we should consider not only the acts that individual committed but also the acts they omitted. Even though in the CIA example no one initiated the wrongful policy, many officials could be blamed for failing to try to halt the practice. Admittedly, there are dangers in adopting a notion of "negative responsibility." [18] One is that such a notion can make individuals culpable for almost anything (since there seems to be no limit to the acts that an individual did not do). But in the context of organizations we can more often point to specific omissions that made a significant difference in the outcome and that are ascribable to specific persons. Patterns of omissions can be predicted and specified in advance.

The force of the second argument, which points to the gap between individual intention and collective outcome, can be blunted if we simply give less weight to intentions than to consequences in assessing moral culpability of officials, at least in two of the senses that "intention" is commonly understood—as motive and as direct goal. It is often hard enough in private life to interpret the motives of persons one knows well; in public life it may be impossible to discover the intentions of officials, especially when the motives of so many of those questioning the motives of officials are themselves questionable. Insofar as we can discover motives, they are relevant in assessing character and may sometimes help in predicting future behavior, but administrative ethics does better to concentrate on actions and results in public life.[19]

What about officials who directly intend only good results but, because of other people's mistakes or other factors they do not foresee, contribute to an unjust or harmful policy? Here the key question is not whether the officials actually foresaw this result, but whether they should have foreseen it.[20] We can legitimately hold public officials to a higher standard than that to which we hold ordinary citizens. We can expect officials to foresee and take into account a wider range of consequences, partly because of the general obligations of public office. Where the welfare of so many are at stake, officials must make exceptional efforts to anticipate consequences of their actions.

Moreover, the nature of organizations itself often forestalls officials from plausibly pleading that they did not foresee what their actions would cause. Organizations tend to produce patterned outcomes; they regularly make the same mistakes in the same ways. While officials may once or twice reasonably claim they should not have been expected to foresee a harmful outcome to which their well-intentioned actions contributed, there must be some (low) limit to the number of times they may use this excuse to escape responsibility. In the example of discrimination in employment, we would say that officials should recognize that their organizational procedures (combined with social forces) are still producing unjust results in personnel decisions; they become partly responsible for the injustice if they do not take steps to overcome it as far as they can.

The requirements of a role insulate an official from blame much less than the earlier argument implied.[21] The example of the New York City fiscal crisis actually tells against that argument as much as for it. Mayor Beame was one of the officials who disclaimed responsibility for the allegedly deceptive accounting practices on the grounds that they were part of organizational routines established many years earlier and could not be changed in the midst of a crisis. But Beame had also served as comptroller and in the budget office during the years when those accounting practices were initiated.[22] In ascribing responsibility to public officials, we should keep in mind that it attaches to persons, not offices. It cannot be entirely determined by any one role a person holds, and it follows a person through time. These features of personal responsibility are sometimes ignored. Public officials are blamed for an immoral (or incompetent) performance in one role but then appear to start with a clean slate once they leave the old job and take a new one. This recycling of discredited public figures is reinforced by the habit of collapsing personal responsibility into role responsibility. Another way that officials may transcend their roles should also be emphasized. Even when a role fully and legitimately constrains what an official may do, personal responsibility need not be completely extinguished. Officials may escape blame for a particular decision, but they do not thereby escape responsibility for seeking to change the constraints of role and structure that helped produce that decision, and they do not escape responsibility for criticizing those constraints. Criticism of one's own past and current performance, and the structures in which that performance takes place, may be the last refuge of moral responsibility in public life.

Administrative ethics is possible—at least, the two major theoretical views that oppose its possibility are not compelling. We are forced to accept neither an ethic of neutrality that would suppress independent moral judgment, nor an ethic of structure that would ignore individual moral agency in organizations. To show that administrative ethics is possible is not of course to show how to make it actual. But understanding why administrative ethics is possible is a necessary step not only toward putting it into practice but also toward giving it meaningful content in practice.

Notes

1. It may be assumed that there is no important philosophical distinction between "ethics" and "morality." Both terms denote the principles of right and wrong in conduct (or the study of such principles). When we refer to the principles of particular professions (e.g., legal ethics or political ethics), "ethics" is the more natural term; and when we refer to personal conduct (e.g., sexual morality), "morality" seems more appropriate. But in their general senses, the terms are fundamentally equivalent. For various definitions of the nature of morality or ethics, see William Frankena, *Ethics*, 2nd ed. (Englewood Cliffs, N.J.: Prentice-Hall, 1973) pp. 1–11; Alan Donagan, *The Theory of Morality* (Chicago: University of Chicago Press, 1977), pp. 1–31; G. J. Warnock, *The Object of Morality* (London: Methuen & Co., 1971), pp. 1–26.

2. Cf. the method of "reflective equilibrium" presented by John Rawls, *A Theory of Justice* (Cambridge: Harvard University Press, 1971), pp. 48–51.

3. For citations and analysis of some writers who adopt part or all of the ethic of neutrality, see Joel L.

Fleishman and Bruce L. Payne (eds.), *Ethical Dilemmas and the Education of Policymakers* (Hastings-on-Hudson, N.Y.: The Hastings Center, 1980), pp. 36–38. Cf. John A. Rohr, *Ethics for Bureaucrats* (New York: Dekker, 1978), pp. 15–47.

4. Cf. George Graham, "Ethical Guidelines for Public Administrators," *Public Administration Review*, vol. 34 (January/February 1974), pp. 90–92.
5. Donald Warwick, "The Ethics of Administrative Discretion," in Joel Fleishman *et al.* (eds.), *Public Duties* (Cambridge: Harvard University Press, 1981), pp. 93–127.
6. Edward Weisband and Thomas M. Franck, *Resignation in Protest* (New York: Penguin, 1976), p. 3.
7. On "complicity," see Thomas E. Hill, "Symbolic Protest and Calculated Silence," *Philosophy & Public Affairs* (Fall 1979), pp. 83–102. For a defense against the charge of moral self-indulgence, see Bernard Williams, *Moral Luck* (Cambridge: Cambridge University Press, 1981), pp. 40–53.
8. For an example of the latter, see Weisband and Franck, p. 46.
9. Cf. Graham, p. 92.
10. James C. Thomson, "How Could Vietnam Happen?" *Atlantic* (April 1968), p. 49. Also see Albert Hirschman, *Exit, Voice, and Loyalty* (Cambridge: Harvard University Press, 1970), pp. 115–119.
11. Thomson, p. 49.
12. Gary J. Greenberg, "Revolt at Justice," in Charles Peters and T. J. Adams (eds.), *Inside the System* (New York: Praeger, 1970), pp. 195–209.
13. See Rawls, pp. 363–391.
14. Dennis F. Thompson, "Moral Responsibility of Public Officials:

The Problem of Many Hands," *American Political Science Review*, vol. 74 (December 1980), pp. 905–916.
15. John Ladd, "Morality and the Ideal of Rationality in Formal Organizations," *Monist*, vol. 54 (October 1970), pp. 488–516.
16. Charles R. Morris, *The Cost of Good Intentions* (New York: W. W. Norton, 1980), pp. 239–240. For some other examples of structuralist analyses, see Herbert Kaufman, *Red Tape* (Washington, D.C.: Brookings, 1977), pp. 27–28; and Richard J. Stillman, *Public Administration: Concepts and Cases*, 2nd ed. (Boston: Houghton-Mifflin, 1980), p. 34.
17. Robert Nozick, *Anarchy, State, and Utopia* (New York: Basic Books, 1974), p. 130.
18. Cf. Bernard Williams, "A Critique of Utilitarianism," in J. J. Smart and Bernard Williams, *Utilitarianism* (Cambridge: Cambridge University Press, 1973), pp. 93–118.
19. But cf. Joel Fleishman, "Self-Interest and Political Integrity," in Fleishman *et al.*, pp. 52–92.
20. But cf. Charles Fried, *Right and Wrong* (Cambridge: Harvard University Press, 1978), esp. pp. 21–22, 26, 28, 202–205. More generally on "intention," see Donagan, *Theory of Morality,* pp. 112–142; and J. L. Mackie, *Ethics* (New York: Penguin, 1977), pp. 203–226.
21. On role responsibility, see H. L. A. Hart, *Punishment and Responsibility* (New York: Oxford University Press, 1968), pp. 212–214; and R. S. Downie, *Roles and Values* (London: Methuen, 1971), pp. 121–145.
22. Dennis F. Thompson, "Moral Responsibility and the New York City Fiscal Crisis, " in Fleishman *et al.*, pp. 266–285.

Why "Good" Managers Make Bad Ethical Choices

Saul W. Gellerman

Why do managers do things that ultimately inflict great harm on their companies, themselves, and people on whose patronage or tolerance their organizations depend? Examples in each day's paper supply ample evidence of the motivations and instincts that underlie corporate misconduct. Although the particulars may vary—from the gruesome dishonesty surrounding asbestos handling to the mundanity of illegal money management—the motivating beliefs are pretty much the same. We may examine them in the context of the corporation, but we know that these feelings are basic throughout society; we find them wherever we go because we take them with us.

When we look more closely at these cases, we can delineate four commonly held rationalizations that can lead to misconduct:

1. A belief that the activity is within reasonable ethical and legal limits—that is, that it is not "really" illegal or immoral.
2. A belief that the activity is in the individual's or the corporation's best interests—that the individual would somehow be expected to undertake the activity.
3. A belief that the activity is "safe" because it will never be found out or publicized; the classic crime-and-punishment issue of discovery.
4. A belief that because the activity helps the company the company will condone it and even protect the person who engages in it.

The idea that an action is not really wrong is an old issue. How far is too far? Exactly where is the line between smart and too smart? Between sharp and shady? Between profit maximization and illegal conduct? The issue is complex: it involves an interplay between top management's goals and middle managers' efforts to interpret those aims.

Put enough people in an ambiguous, ill-defined situation, and some will conclude that whatever hasn't been labeled specifically wrong must be OK—especially if they are rewarded for certain acts.

Top executives seldom ask their subordinates to do things that both of them know are against the law or imprudent. But company leaders sometimes leave things unsaid or give the impression that there are things they don't want to know about. In other words, they can seem, whether deliberately or otherwise, to be distancing themselves from their subordinates' tactical decisions in order to keep their own hands clean if things go awry. Often they lure ambitious lower level managers by implying that rich rewards await those who can produce certain results—and that the methods for achieving them will not be examined too closely.

How can managers avoid crossing a line that is seldom precise? Unfortunately, most know that they have overstepped it only when they have gone too far. They have no reliable guidelines about what will be overlooked or tolerated or what will be condemned or attacked. When managers must operate in murky borderlands, their most reliable guideline is an old principle: when in doubt, don't.

That may seem like a timid way to run a business. One could argue that if it actually took hold among the middle managers who run most companies, it might take the enterprise out of free enterprise. But there is a difference between taking a worthwhile economic risk and risking an illegal act to make more money.

The difference between becoming a success and becoming a statistic lies in knowledge—including self-knowledge—not daring. Contrary to popular mythology, managers are not paid to take risks; they are paid to know which risks are worth taking. Also, maximizing profits is a company's second priority, not its first. The first is ensuring its survival.

All managers risk giving too much because of what their companies demand from them. But the same superiors who keep pressing you to do more, or to do it better, or faster, or less expensively, will turn on you should you cross that fuzzy line between right and wrong. They will blame you for exceeding instructions or for ignoring their warnings. The smartest managers already know that the best answer to the question, "How far is too far?" is don't try to find out.

Turning to the second reason why people take risks that get their companies into trouble, believing that unethical conduct is in a

Ethics and decision making

Decisions may pose ethical dilemmas whenever profit or personal gain might reasonably cause harm or loss for another. Laura Nash of the Harvard Business School lists the following 12 questions managers should ask when making decisions:

1. Have you defined the problem accurately?
2. How would you define the problem if you stood on the other side of the fence?
3. How did this situation occur in the first place?
4. To whom and to what do you give your loyalty as a person and as a member of the corporation?
5. What is your intention in making this decision?
6. How does this intention compare with the probable results?
7. Whom could your decision or action injure?
8. Can you discuss the problem with the affected parties before you make your decision?
9. Are you confident that your position will be as valid over a long period of time as it seems now?
10. Could you disclose without qualm your decision or action to your boss, your CEO, the board of directors, your family, society as a whole?
11. What is the symbolic potential of your action if understood? If misunderstood?
12. Under what conditions would you allow exceptions to your stand?

You can't readily answer any of these questions with black and white pronouncements: there are too many gray areas and the issues are complex. Managers can't always know with certainty what might result from their decisions since each case may carry unforeseen ramifications. But discussing Nash's list of questions in a management-development session will certainly provide managers and executives with a spirited educational experience.

Source: Reprinted by permission of the *Harvard Business Review*. An exhibit from "Ethics Without the Sermon" by Laura L. Nash (November-December 1981). Copyright © 1981 by the President and Fellows of Harvard College; all rights reserved. As used in Herb Genfan, "Formalizing Business Ethics," *Training and Development Journal*, November 1987.

person's or corporation's best interests nearly always results from a parochial view of what those interests are. For example, Alpha Industries, a Massachusetts manufacturer of microwave equipment, paid $57,000 to a Raytheon manager, ostensibly for a marketing report. Air force investigators charged that the report was a ruse to cover a bribe: Alpha wanted subcontracts that the Raytheon manager supervised. But those contracts ultimately cost Alpha a lot more than they paid for the report. After the company was indicted for bribery, its contracts were suspended and its profits promptly vanished. Alpha wasn't unique in this transgression: in 1984, the Pentagon suspended 453 other companies for violating procurement regulations.

Ambitious managers look for ways to attract favorable attention, something to distinguish them from other people. So they try to outperform their peers. Some may see that it is not difficult to look remarkably good in the short run by avoiding things that pay off only in the long run. For example, you can skimp on maintenance or training or customer service, and you can get away with it—for a while.

The sad truth is that many managers have been promoted on the basis of "great" results obtained in just those ways, leaving unfortunate successors to inherit the inevitable whirlwind. Since this is not necessarily a just world, the problems that such people create are not always traced back to them. Companies cannot afford to be hoodwinked in this way. They must be concerned with more than just results. They have to look very hard at how results are obtained.

This brings up another dilemma: management quite naturally hopes that any of its borderline actions will be overlooked or at least interpreted charitably if noticed. Companies must accept human nature for what it is and protect themselves with watchdogs to sniff out possible misdeeds.

An independent auditing agency that reports to outside directors can play such a role. It can provide a less comfortable, but more convincing, review of how management's successes are achieved. The discomfort can be considered inexpensive insurance and serve to remind all employees that the real interests of the company are served by honest conduct in the first place.

The third reason why a risk is taken, believing that one can probably get away with it, is perhaps the most difficult to deal with because it's often true. A great deal of proscribed behavior escapes detection.

We know that conscience alone does not deter everyone. For example, First National Bank of Boston pleaded guilty to laundering satchels of $20 bills worth $1.3 billion. Thousands of satchels must have passed through the bank's doors without incident before the scheme was detected. That kind of heavy, unnoticed traffic breeds complacency.

How can we deter wrongdoing that is unlikely to be detected? Make it more likely to be detected. Had today's "discovery" process—in which plaintiff's attorneys can comb through a company's records to look for incriminating evidence—been in use when Manville concealed the evidence on asbestosis, there probably would have been no cover-up. Mindful of the likelihood of detection, Manville would have chosen a different course and could very well be thriving today without the protection of the bankruptcy courts.

The most effective deterrent is not to increase the severity of punishment for those caught but to heighten the perceived probability of being caught in the first place. For example, police have found that parking an empty patrol car at locations where motorists often exceed the speed limit reduces the frequency of speeding. Neighborhood "crime watch" signs that people display decrease burglaries.

Simply increasing the frequency of audits and spot checks is a deterrent, especially when combined with three other simple techniques: scheduling audits irregularly, making at least half of them unannounced, and setting up some checkups soon after others. But frequent spot checks cost more than big sticks, a fact that raises the question of which approach is more cost-effective.

A common managerial error is to assume that because frequent audits uncover little behavior that is out of line, less frequently, and therefore less costly, auditing is sufficient. But this condition overlooks the important deterrent effect of frequent checking. The point is to prevent misconduct, not just to catch it.

A trespass detected should not be dealt with discreetly. Managers should announce the misconduct and how the individuals involved were punished. Since the main deterrent to illegal or unethical behavior is the perceived probability of detection, managers should make an example of people who are detected.

Let's look at the fourth reason why corporate misconduct tends to occur, a belief that the company will condone actions that are taken in its interest and will even protect the managers responsible. The question we have to deal with here is, How do we keep company loyalty from going berserk?

That seems to be what happened at Manville, where a small group of executives and a succession of corporate medical directors kept the facts about the lethal qualities of asbestos from becoming public knowledge for decades; and they managed to live with that knowledge. And at Manville, the company—or really, the company's senior management—did condone their decision and protect those employees.

Something similar seems to have happened at General Electric. When one of its missile projects ran up costs greater than the air force had agreed to pay, middle managers surreptitiously shifted those costs to projects that were still operating under budget. In this case, the loyalty that ran amok was primarily to the division: managers want their units' results to look good. But GE, with one of the finest reputations in U.S. industry, was splattered with scandal and paid a fine of $1.04 million.

One of the most troubling aspects of the GE case is the company's admission that those involved were thoroughly familiar with the company's ethical standards before the incident took place. This suggests that the practice of declaring codes of ethics and teaching them to managers is not enough to deter unethical conduct. Something stronger is needed.

Top management has a responsibility to exert a moral force within the company. Senior executives are responsible for drawing the line between loyalty to the company and action against the laws and values of the society in which the company must operate. Further, because that line can be obscured in the heat of the moment, the line has to be drawn well short of where reasonable men and women could begin to suspect that their rights had been violated. The company has to react long before a prosecutor, for instance, would have a strong enough case to seek an indictment.

Executives have a right to expect loyalty from employees against competitors and detractors, but not loyalty against the law, or against common morality, or against society itself. Managers must warn employees that a disservice to customers, and especially to innocent bystanders, cannot be a service to the company. Finally, and most important of all, managers must stress that excuses of company loyalty will not be accepted for acts that place its good name in jeopardy. To put it bluntly, superiors must make it clear that employees who harm other people allegedly for the company's benefit will be fired.

The most extreme examples of corporate misconduct were due, in hindsight, to managerial failures. A good way to avoid management oversights is to subject the control mechanisms themselves to periodic surprise audits, perhaps as a function of the board of directors. The point is to make sure that internal audits and controls are functioning as planned. It's a case of inspecting the inspectors and taking the necessary steps to keep the controls working efficiently. Harold Geneen, former head of ITT, has suggested that the board should have an independent staff, something analogous to the Government Accounting Office, which reports to the legislative rather than the executive branch. In the end, it is up to top management to send a clear and pragmatic message to all employees that good ethics is still the foundation of good business.

PART 2

Ethical Decision Making

Ethical Managers Make Their Own Rules

Sir Adrian Cadbury

In 1900 Queen Victoria sent a decorative tin with a bar of chocolate inside to all of her soldiers who were serving in South Africa. These tins still turn up today, often complete with their contents, a tribute to the collecting instinct. At the time, the order faced my grandfather with an ethical dilemma. He owned and ran the second-largest chocolate company in Britain, so he was trying harder and the order meant additional work for the factory. Yet he was deeply and publicly opposed to the Anglo-Boer War. He resolved the dilemma by accepting the order, but carrying it out at cost. He therefore made no profit out of what he saw as an unjust war, his employees benefited from the additional work, the soldiers received their royal present, and I am still sent the tins.

My grandfather was able to resolve the conflict between the decision best for his business and his personal code of ethics because he and his family owned the firm which bore their name. Certainly his dilemma would have been more acute if he had had to take into account the interests of outside shareholders, many of whom would no doubt have been in favor both of the war and of profiting from it. But even so, not all my grandfather's ethical dilemmas could be as straightforwardly resolved.

So strongly did my grandfather feel about the South African War that he acquired and financed the only British newspaper which opposed it. He was also against gambling, however, and so he tried to run the paper without any references to horse racing. The effect on the newspaper's circulation was such that he had to choose between his ethical beliefs. He decided, in the end, that it was more important that the paper's voice be heard as widely as possible than that gambling should thereby receive some mild encouragement. The decision was doubtless a relief to those working on the paper and to its readers.

The way my grandfather settled these two clashes of principle brings out some practical points about ethics and business decisions. In the first place, the possibility that ethical and commercial considerations will conflict has always faced those who run companies. It is not a new problem. The difference now is that a more widespread and critical interest is being taken in our decisions and in the ethical judgments which lie behind them.

Secondly, as the newspaper example demonstrates, ethical signposts do not always point in the same direction. My grandfather had to choose between opposing a war and condoning gambling. The rule that it is best to tell the truth often runs up against the rule that we should not hurt people's feelings unnecessarily. There is no simple, universal formula for solving ethical problems. We have to choose from our own codes of conduct whichever rules are appropriate to the case in hand; the outcome of those choices makes us who we are.

Lastly, while it is hard enough to resolve dilemmas when our personal rules of conduct conflict, the real difficulties arise when we have to make decisions which affect the interests of others. We can work out what weighting to give to our own rules through trial and error. But business decisions require us to do the same for others by allocating weights to all the conflicting interests which may be involved. Frequently, for example, we must balance the interests of employees against those of shareholders. But even that sounds more straightforward than it really is, because there may well be differing views among the shareholders, and the interests of past, present, and future employees are unlikely to be identical.

Eliminating ethical considerations from business decisions would simplify the management task, and Milton Friedman has urged something of the kind in arguing that the interaction between business and society should be left to the political process. "Few trends could so thoroughly undermine the very foundation of our free society," he writes in *Capitalism and Freedom*," as the acceptance by corporate officials of a social responsibility other than to make as much money for their shareholders as possible."

But the simplicity of this approach is deceptive. Business is part of the social system and we cannot isolate the economic elements of major decisions from their social consequences. So there are no simple rules. Those who make business decisions have to assess the economic and social consequences of their actions as best as they can and come to their conclusions on limited information and in a limited time.

As will already be apparent, I use the word ethics to mean the guidelines or rules of conduct by which we aim to live. It is, of course, foolhardy to write about ethics at all, because you lay yourself open to the charge of taking up a position of moral superiority, of failing to practice what you preach, or both. I am not in a position to preach nor am I promoting a specific code of conduct. I believe, however, that it is useful to all of us who are responsible for business decisions to acknowledge the part which ethics plays in those decisions and to encourage discussion of how best to combine commercial and ethical judgments. Most business decisions involve some degree of ethical judgment; few can be taken solely on the basis of arithmetic.

While we refer to a company as having a set of standards, that is a convenient shorthand. The people who make up the company are responsible for its conduct and it is their collective actions which determine the company's standards. The ethical standards of a company are judged by its actions, not by pious statements of intent put out in its name. This does not mean that those who head companies should not set down what they believe their companies stand for— hard though that is to do. The character of a company is a matter of importance to those in it, to those who do business with it, and to those who are considering joining it.

What matters most, however, is where we stand as individual managers and how we behave when faced with decisions which require us to combine ethical and commercial judgments. In approaching such decisions, I believe it is helpful to go through two steps. The first is to determine, as precisely as we can, what our personal rules of conduct are. This does not mean drawing up a list of virtuous notions, which will probably end up as a watered-down version of the Scriptures without their literary merit. It does men looking back at decisions we have made and working out from there what our rules actually are. The aim is to avoid confusing ourselves and everyone else by declaring one set of principles and acting on another. Our ethics are expressed in our actions, which is why they are usually clearer to others than to ourselves.

Once we know where we stand personally we can move on to the second step, which is to think through who else will be affected by the decision and how we should weight their interest in it. Some interests will be represented by well-organized groups; others will have no one to put their case. If a factory manager is negotiating a wage claim with employee representatives, their remit is to look after the interests of those who are already employed. Yet the effect of the wage settlement on the factory's costs may well determine whether new employees are likely to be taken on. So the manager cannot ignore the interest of potential employees in the outcome of the negotiation, even though that interest is not represented at the bargaining table.

The rise of organized interest groups makes it doubly important that managers consider the arguments of everyone with a legitimate interest in a decision's outcome. Interest groups seek publicity to promote their causes and they have the advantage of being single-minded: they are against building an airport on a certain site, for example, but take no responsibility for finding a better alternative. This narrow focus gives pressure groups a debating advantage against managements, which cannot evade the responsibility for taking decisions in the same way.

In *The Hard Problems of Management*, Mark Pastin has perceptively referred to this phenomenon as the ethical superiority of the uninvolved, and there is a good deal of it about. Pressure groups are skilled at seizing the high moral ground and arguing that our judgment as managers is at best biased and at worst influenced soley by private gain because we have a direct commercial interest in the outcome of our decisions. But as managers we are also responsible for arriving at business decisions which take account of all the interests concerned; the uninvolved are not.

At times the campaign to persuade companies to divest themselves of their South African subsidiaries has exemplified this kind of ethical high-handedness. Apartheid is abhorrent politically, socially, and morally. Those who argue that they can exert some influence on the direction of change by staying put believe this as sincerely as those who favor divestment. Yet many anti-apartheid campaigners reject the proposition that both sides have the same end in view. From their perspective it is self-evident that the only ethical course of action is for companies to wash their hands of the problems of South Africa by selling out.

Managers cannot be so self-assured. In deciding what weight to give to the arguments for and against divestment, we must consider who has what at stake in the outcome of the decision. The employees of a South African subsidiary have the most direct stake, as the decision affects their future; they are also the group whose voice is least likely to be heard outside South Africa. The shareholders have at stake any loss on divestment, against which must be balanced any gain in the value of their shares through severing the South African connection. The divestment lobby is the one group for whom the decision is costless either way.

What is clear even from this limited analysis is that there is no general answer to the question of whether companies should sell their South African subsidiaries or not. Pressure to reduce complicated issues to straightforward alternatives, one of which is right and the other wrong, is a regrettable sign of the times. But boards are rarely presented with two clearly opposed alternatives. Companies faced with the same issues will therefore properly come to different conclusions and their decisions may alter over time.

A less contentious divestment decision faced my own company when we decided to sell our foods division. Because the division was mainly a U.K. business with regional brands, it did not fit the company's strategy, which called for concentrating resources behind our confectionery and soft drinks brands internationally. But it was an attractive business in its own right and the decision to sell prompted both a management bid and external offers.

Employees working in the division strongly supported the management bid and made their views felt. In this instance, they were the best organized interest group and they had more information available to them to back their case than any of the other parties involved. What they had at stake was also very clear.

From the shareholders' point of view, the premium over asset value offered by the various bidders was a key aspect of the decision. They also had an interest in seeing the deal completed without regulatory delays and without diverting too much management attention from the ongoing business. In addition, the way in which the successful bidder would guard the brand name had to be considered, since the division would take with it products carrying the parent company's name.

In weighing the advantages and disadvantages of the various offers, the board considered all the groups, consumers among them, who would be affected by the sale. But our main task was to reconcile the interests of the employees and of the shareholders. (The more, of course, we can encourage employees to become shareholders, the closer together the interests of these two stakeholders will be brought.) The division's management upped its bid in the face of outside competition, and after due deliberation we decided to sell to the management team, believing that this choice best balanced the diverse interests at stake.

Companies whose activities are international face an additional complication in taking their decisions. They aim to work to the same standards of business conduct wherever they are to behave as good corporate citizens of the countries in which they trade. But the two aims are not always compatible: promotion on merit may be the rule of the company and promotion by seniority the custom of the country. In addition, while the financial arithmetic on which companies base their decisions is generally accepted, what is considered ethical varies among cultures.

If what would be considered corruption in the company's home territory is an accepted business practice elsewhere, how are local managers expected to act? Companies could do business only in countries in which they feel ethically at home, provided always that their shareholders take the same view. But this approach could prove unduly restrictive, and there is also a certain arrogance in dismissing foreign codes of conduct without considering why they may be different. If companies find, for example, that they have to pay customs officers in another country just to do their job, it may be that the state is simply transferring its responsibilities to the private sector as an alternative to using taxation less efficiently to the same end.

Nevertheless, this example brings us to one of the most common ethical issues companies face—how far to go in buying business? What payments are legitimate for companies to make to win orders and, the reverse side of that coin, when do gifts to employees become bribes? I use two rules of thumb to test whether a payment is acceptable from the company's point of view: Is the payment on the face of the invoice? Would it embarrass the recipient to have the gift mentioned in the company newspaper?

The first test ensures that all payments, however unusual they may seem, are recorded and go through the books. The second is aimed at distinguishing bribes from gifts, a definition which depends on the size of the gift and the influence it is likely to have on the recipient. The value of a case of whiskey to me would be limited, because I only take it as medicine. We know ourselves whether a gift is acceptable or not and we know that others will know if they are aware of the nature of the gift.

As for payment on the face of the invoice, I have found it a useful general rule precisely because codes of conduct do vary around the world. It has legitimized some otherwise unlikely company payments, to the police in one country, for example, and to the official planning authorities in another, but all went through the books and were audited. Listing a payment on the face of the invoice may not be a sufficient ethical test, but it is a necessary one; payments outside the company's system are corrupt and corrupting.

The logic behind these rules of thumb is that openness and ethics go together and that actions are unethical if they will not stand scrutiny. Openness in arriving at decisions reflects the same logic. It gives those with an interest in a particular decision the chance to make their views known and opens to argument the basis on which the decision is finally taken. This in turn enables the decision makers to learn from experience and to improve their powers of judgment.

Openness is also, I believe, the best way to disarm outside suspicion of companies' motives and actions. Disclosure is not a panacea for improving the relations between business and society, but the willingness to operate an open system is the foundation of those relations. Business needs to be open to the views of society and open in return about its own activities; this is essential for the establishment of trust.

For the same reasons, as managers we need to be candid when making decisions about other people. Dr. Johnson reminds us that when it comes to lapidary inscriptions, "no man is upon oath." But what should be disclosed in references, in fairness to those looking for work and to those who are considering employing them?

The simplest rule would seem to be that we should write the kind of reference we would wish to read. Yet "do as you would be done by" says nothing about ethics. The actions which result from applying it could be ethical or unethical, depending on the standards of the initiator. The rule could be adapted to help managers determine their ethical standards, however, by reframing it as a question: If you did business with yourself, how ethical would you think you were?

Anonymous letters accusing an employee of doing something discreditable create another context in which candor is the wisest course. Such letters cannot by definition be answered, but they convey a message to those who receive them, however warped or unfair the message may be. I normally destroy these letters, but tell the person concerned what has been said. This conveys the disregard I attach to nameless allegation, but preserves the rule of openness. From a practical point of view, it serves as a warning if there is anything in the allegations; from an ethical point of view, the degree to which my judgment of the person may not be prejudiced is known between us.

The last aspect of ethics in business decisions I want to discuss concerns our responsibility for the level of employment; what can or should companies do about the provision of jobs? This issue is of immediate concern to European managers because unemployment is higher in Europe than it is in the United States and the net number of new jobs created has been much lower. It comes to the fore whenever companies face decisions which require a trade-off between increasing efficiency and reducing numbers employed.

If you believe, as I do, that the primary purpose of a company is to satisfy the needs of its customers and to do so profitably, the creation of jobs cannot be the company's goal as well. Satisfying customers requires companies to compete in the marketplace, and so we cannot opt out of introducing new technology, for example, to preserve jobs. To do so would be to deny consumers the benefits of progress, to short-change the shareholders, and in the longer run to put the jobs of everyone in the company at risk. What destroys jobs certainly and permanently is the failure to be competitive.

Experience says that the introduction of new technology creates more jobs that it eliminates, in ways which cannot be forecast.

It may do so, however, only after a time lag, and those displaced may not, through lack of skills, be able to take advantage of the new opportunities when they arise. Nevertheless, the company's prime responsibility to everyone who has a stake in it is to retain its competitive edge, even if this means a loss of jobs in the short run.

Where companies do have a social responsibility, however, is in how we manage that situation, how we smooth the path of technological change. Companies are responsible for the timing of such changes and we are in a position to involve those who will be affected by the way in which those changes are introduced. We also have a vital resource in our capacity to provide training, so that continuing employees can take advantage of change and those who may lose their jobs can more readily find new ones.

In the United Kingdom, an organization called Business in the Community has been established to encourage the formation of new enterprises. Companies have backed it with cash and with secondments. The secondment of able managers to worthwhile institutions is a particularly effective expression of concern, because the ability to manage is such a scarce resource. Through Business in the Community we can create jobs collectively, even if we cannot do so individually, and it is clearly in our interest to improve the economic and social climate in this way.

Throughout, I have been writing about the responsibilities of those who head companies and my emphasis has been on taking decisions, because that is what directors and managers are appointed to do. what concerns me is that too often the public pressures which are put on companies in the name of ethics encourage their boards to put off decisions or to wash their hands of problems. There may well be commercial reasons for those choices, but there are rarely ethical ones. The ethical bases on which decisions are arrived at will vary among companies, but shelving those decisions is likely to be the last ethical course.

The company which takes drastic action in order to survive is more likely to be criticized publicly than the one which fails to grasp the nettle and gradually but inexorably declines. There is always a temptation to postpone difficult decisions, but it is not in society's interests that hard choices should be evaded because of public clamor or the possibility of legal action. Companies need to be encouraged to take the decisions which face them; the responsibility for providing that encouragement rests with society as a whole.

Society sets the ethical framework within which those who run companies have to work out their own codes of conduct. Responsibility for decisions, therefore, runs both ways. Business has to take account of its responsibilities to society in coming to its decisions, but society has to accept its responsibilities for setting the standards against which those decisions are made.

Ethical
Styles

————— Robert C. Solomon and Kristine R. Hanson

One of the most important but least often addressed aspects of ethics is the difference among ethical styles. It is a problem that surfaces in almost every discussion of actual cases, whether in business school or in the boardroom, whether the topic is South Africa or advertising for children on television. Different people have different premises, different ways of arguing, different ways of doing the right thing. There are ethical styles just as there are social styles and styles of management and marketing. A clash of ethical styles can be far more disruptive and destructive to business tranquillity than differences of opinion or clashes of personality. In a conflict of ethical styles, each party typically thinks the other "immoral"—or worse. Negotiation breaks down, not because there is no common point of interest but because there is not even agreement on the kinds of interests that are relevant to the case.

The most familiar clash of ethical styles—one that emerges in almost every management context—is the sort of seemingly irresolvable conflict that we find between Manny K., who feels absolutely constrained by the letter of the law, and John Stuart, who is more concerned with the practical specifics of the case at hand. For Manny K., it does not matter that the rule in question is outdated or impractical. It does not matter that it became a matter of law or policy under another administration, which is now out of office. It does not matter that the rule will no doubt be changed someday. Manny K. believes that one should obey rules, whatever their origins and whatever the consequences. Any other way of thinking, from his standpoint, is amoral.

John Stuart, on the other hand, is a self-consciously practical person. Rules serve a purpose, a function, and they are to be obeyed just because—but only because—they serve that purpose or function. A rule that proves to be impractical no longer deserves our respect or obedience. A rule that was formulated under very different circumstances or was legislated by a different administration should be carefully scrutinized and not given too much weight. John Stuart makes his decisions on the sole ground that a certain course of action has the best consequences for everyone involved. If that fits the rules (as it usually does), then so much the better. If it does not, then so much the worse for the rules—and so much too for that stubborn Manny K., who for some unfathomable reason refuses to see the point.

Manny K. considers John Stuart to be nothing but an amoral opportunist, a man who does not respect authority and the rules. John Stuart considers Manny K. to be utterly unreasonable and impractical, if not "impossible." When general utility conflicts with an established rule, John and Manny are certain to misunderstand each other. There can be no compromise, because each of them considers his own position to be beyond question and cannot understand the other, except, perhaps, as pathology.

Why has so familiar a scenario found so minimal a role in studies of organizational behavior and business ethics? Ethical styles have been ignored by business writers because we tend to assume that ethical principles, unlike personalities and public policies, are universal and nonnegotiable. One executive interrupted at the beginning of one of our seminars and, crossing his arms in defiance, challenged the very purpose of our discussion, saying, "There is right, and there is wrong. There is nothing more to discuss, in business or anywhere else." We responded, of course, with a case designed to bring out the conflict of established rules with practical necessities, and the John Stuarts in the group soon rose to the occa-

---

Ethical styles

1.	Rule-bound	obedience to law, rule, principle
2.	Utilitarian	consequences for everybody
3.	Loyalist	the company first
4.	Prudent	our long-term advantage
5.	Virtuous	character, reputation are all-important
6.	Intuitive	spontaneous judgments
7.	Empathetic	"how must he feel?"
8.	Darwinian	whoever survives is right

sion, making our point for us. One of the more destructive legacies of
our Judeo-Christian tradition in ethics is that it tends to encourage
dogmatic and intolerant thinking precisely where understanding
and tolerance are most necessary.

There are a number of ethical styles, of which Manny K. and
John Stuart exemplify but two. There are styles that emphasize
painful wrestling with problems and styles that rely on sheer intuition. There are styles that emphasize pity and compassion, and
there are styles that stress the importance of being detached and
objective. Not every attitude in ethics is an ethical style, of course.
Being immoral is not an ethical style. Selfishness, despite its occasional vogue as an "enlightened" ethics, is not an ethical style. There
are, however, many styles of ethics in business. Here are eight of
them:

1. Rule-bound Thinking and acting on the basis of rules and
principles, paying only secondary regard to circumstances or exceptions (Manny K).

2. Utilitarian Weighing probable consequences, both to the
company and to the public well-being. Principles are important only
as rules of thumb. "The greatest good for the greatest number of
people" is the ultimate test for any action or decision (John Stuart).

3. Loyalist Evaluating all decisions first in terms of benefit to
the company and its reputation. The concern with reputation (moti-
vated by one's own pride in the company) also ensures general conformity to laws and principles and concern with the company's role
in the larger social picture. (Also called "company man.")

4. Prudent Weighing probable consequences to oneself and one's
own concerns but always including long-range considerations of
company reputation, public trust, customer and supplier relations,
ability to obtain loans, etc. Prudence is not the same as selfishness
or crude self-interest (though it is sometimes called "enlightened
self-interest") since it has built into it the mutual dependence of
one's own interests and company interests. The primary difference
between the prudent strategist, the loyalist, and the utilitarian is
that the first is concerned primarily with himself and only second-
arily with the rest of the world; the second is concerned primarily
with the well-being of the company without special regard for him-
or herself. The utilitarian takes the broader social view and, though
naturally concerned with his or her own and his or her company's
success, thinks in terms of the overall good. The prudent strategist
lives on the border between ethics and self-interest and unlike the
loyalist and the utilitarian is not unlikely to give up his tentative

ethical stance under pressure or conflict. A special case is the person Maccoby calls the "gamesman," whose ethical commitment might be said to be limited to the "rules of the business game," within which the primary motivations are to be challenged and to win, without respect for the rules he has to obey (in order to play) and without regard for the actual consequences of his actions.

5. Virtuous Every action is measured in terms of its reflection of one's character or the company reputation, without immediate regard to consequences and often without paying much attention to general principles. The virtuous style can vary in both scope and method; it can be identical in its concerns to the company concerns of the loyalist, or it can encompass the social world—as in the actions of some of the great business philanthropists. It can pride itself on obedience to the rules, or it can pride itself for its unerring intuitions, but it is one's own virtue that is the source of pride rather than the autonomous motive to obey the rules, for example.

6. Intuitive Making decisions on the basis of "conscience" and without deliberation, argument, or reasons, the intelligence of which may not be immediately apparent. Intuitive thinkers tend to be extremely impatient with more deliberative, rule-bound, and utilitarian types. It is a style that usually flourishes only at the top of the decision-making hierarchy, and continued success (by moral, utilitarian, and prudential standards) is essential, since errors in intuition, unlike errors in deliberation and strategy, cannot be readily explained or rationalized.

7. Empathetic Following one's feelings, in particular, feelings of sympathy and compassion. "Putting oneself in the other's place" is the modus operandi of the sentimental style, whether the "other" be a competitor ("How would we like it if he . . .") or a customer ("Suppose you found yourself stuck with . . .").

8. Darwinian Whoever survives must be right. In some versions, this is clearly not an ethical position (e.g., "If we win, we're right, but if they win, we were wronged"). But a consistent Darwinian fully accepts the possibility and even the desirability of his or her own failure to a superior competitor, without complaint.

Ethics is thinking in terms of the "large picture," not ignoring or neglecting one's own interests and well-being (a faulty view of ethics) but not overemphasizing one's own interests either. When, as is usual, one's own interests coincide with company interests, the distinction does not even arise (which is why the prudential strategist can be tentatively included in the list of ethical styles). And when, which is also usual, the (long-term) well-being of the company coincides with its positive contributions to society, there need be no distinction made between company loyalty and the more general good (which is why the loyalist has an ethical style rather than just a sociological attachment). In fact, in such amiable circum-

---

Ascertaining your ethical style

(A = agree, D = disagree)

_____ 1. "It really bothers me when someone ignores or breaks one of the company rules. It's the same kind of feeling I get when I see someone run a red light, even if no one else is on the road."

_____ 2. "I get so irritated when one of the bureaucrats at the office insists on following the rules when there just isn't any point to it. I mean, rules are made to be broken, right? At least as long as no one gets hurt. The important thing is productivity, not kowtowing to bureaucrats."

_____ 3. "My feeling is that anyone who can't stand behind company policy—100%—just shouldn't be here. If they think that the company is doing something wrong, they should quietly leave. Otherwise, they ought to support it."

_____ 4. "You've always got to ask 'How will this benefit us in the long run?' I don't believe in short-term solutions. But I do believe that if we can make our company prosper over the long haul, it will be best for everyone—and especially for us. I'm not saying we should be selfish, but no one is going to prosper if we sacrifice ourselves."

_____ 5. "I always ask 'Will I be able to look at myself in the mirror in the morning and say, "I'm proud of you"?' It's the same with the company. I'd hate to have to explain to my friends that, sure, the project has given us a black eye in the press, but we stand to make nearly a quarter billion on it. You want to make an impressive profit to bolster your reputation—with the board and the stockholders, with your friends and family. If you sacrifice your reputation, what's the point of making money?"

_____ 6. "I just know when something's wrong. It's as if I can *smell* it. Don't ask me how I know, but I'm hardly ever wrong."

_____ 7. "I always put myself in the other guy's shoes. It's not that I'll always give in if he's hurt, but I have to know how he feels. If it's a customer who's bought a bum product, I think of how I'd feel cheated if it were me. If it's a competitor who's lost a fair fight, I still ask 'How does he feel?' but at least I know he doesn't (or shouldn't) feel cheated."

_____ 8. "Rockefeller, Frick, Mellon, Carnegie, Vanderbilt—I mean, you're not talking about nice guys who fought a clean fight. They did whatever they had to, and they won. History says that they're right, and it's the same with all of us now. No one ever made the history books by being right in business and going broke."

stances, ethical styles overlap or remain hidden from view; "business as usual" usually takes ethical considerations for granted (which is not to be confused, as it so often is, with the supposed irrelevance of ethical considerations in business). It is in times of conflict or crisis that differences in ethical styles become prominent, and it is in those times that such differences must be understood and negotiated instead of—as happens so often—being allowed to make a bad situation that much more explosive.

We said that each of these styles has its characteristic advantages and disadvantages; for example, the lack of practical flexibility in rule-bound moral thinking, the sometimes impossible complexity of utilitarian calculations, and the untrustworthy (because only tentative) ethical dependability of the prudential strategist. But this is not the place to explore these in detail; rather we wish to stress the variety of ethical styles, each of which defines its own criteria for right thinking (e.g., in the rule-bound style, thinking about applying the right rules; in the intuitive style, minimal thinking) and right action (good for the company, good for society, good for others). Understanding the differences and resolving conflicts among ethical styles can sometimes be as important and as difficult as resolving the ethical problems themselves.

An Ethical Framework for Human Resource Decision Making

Debra W. Stewart

The core personnel management functions of the line manager are to select, develop, and evaluate people. Historically, public sector managers accepted implicit norms which formed the basis for these personnel management decisions. As Herbert Simon pointed out in his perceptive analysis of administrative decision making, such norms established the "decision premises" for the manager.[1] These premises reflected contemporary prevailing values and evolved with those values, a process well documented in Herbert Kaufman's classic *Public Administration Review* article, "Administrative Decentralization and Political Power." Kaufman describes a cycle, with shifts in values and outlook over time. ". . . [T]he administrative history of our governmental machinery can be construed as a succession of shifts . . . each brought about by a change in emphasis among three values: representativeness, politically neutral competence, and executive leadership."[2] To Kaufman, this process is part of the normal expression of interest in the American political system. Central to Kaufman's analysis is the assumption that while no value is ever totally ignored, one value will always transcend others. The new emphasis comes to displace an earlier emphasis as a pressure experienced by managers.

While Kaufman's model works well to describe administrative history in American public service, observers today note a change. Rather than one interest gaining marked ascendance, interests seem to establish footholds that prevent displacement. Thus, new interests emerge to flourish simultaneously with old interests, each pressing competing claims on government decision-making procedures and practices. It is in this context that we examine the personnel activities of the line manager.

In performing the core personnel management functions of selecting, developing and evaluating people, the line manager today is asked to act on decision premises rooted in three distinct criteria. These premises emerge from different historical contexts, are advocated by different societal groups, place competing claims before the decision maker, and each leads ultimately toward the institutionalization of practices which may impede successful achievement of important goals which other groups promote. The challenge of the 1980s is to balance competing claims, deferring to the just interests of all parties through management strategies which maintain the flexibility necessary to respond to those evolving interests. The scholar's task is to help administrators find the best path toward that objective.

The collective negotiations premise

... Though managers often see the collective negotiations process as an exercise in power politics seldom regulated by moral principles, "rights" issues remain the hidden dimension underlying all labor-management relations. A straightforward rationale gives rise to the notion of a right to negotiate collectively. In capitalism individuals enter into contracts with employers to provide labor in exchange for money. But as individuals, employees are at a disadvantage in the interactions. In order to give the employee the power necessary to ensure fairness in the negotiation with the employer about the nature of the employment contract and the interpretation of this contract, collective bargaining rights are necessary. In fact, to make capitalism work as a fair system, some such provisions are essential.

Students of American politics recognize this as a fundamentally pluralist political argument. It is consistent with pluralist democratic theory for the employee unions (interest groups) to organize politically and to bargain with management (government officials) to advance their own interests. The ideal behind the practice is that sharing in decision making that affects one's livelihood is a basic human right.[3] ...

The merit premise

... As defined here, merit means employment actions based upon qualification, with resources being allocated to the best candidates through a selection process consisting of competitive tests. As a norm for regulating public managerial practices, merit was born of a reform ideology based upon three propositions:

1. Government employment was an open arena where the best could prove themselves.
2. Only the best would produce efficient administration.
3. Public interest is served if the best govern.[4]

... As a decision premise, merit embodies basic Aristotelian notions of procedural justice, which call for treating equals equally and treating unequals unequally. The way to ensure that merit is the regulating principle in employment actions is to institutionalize it through establishing civil service examinations and vertical advancement practices. The efficiency and validity of selection methods become the focus of attention; their value is confirmed by their capacity to distinguish employees or applicants with the greatest merit.

The current day spokespersons for the [merit premise] are the personnel professionals. Glenn Stahl voices this value orientation clearly: "the merit method has no substitutes in providing the conditions of competence and continuity that are essential to the operation of the complex administrative machine of modern government."[5] Frederick Mosher notes that merit achieves this purpose both negatively, by eliminating irrelevant considerations in assessing an employee, and positively, by measuring relative capacity to perform a specific type of work.[6]

Tension between the first two decision premises discussed, collective negotiations and merit, is clear.... The public administration literature called attention to the diverse implications of these two premises nearly 20 years ago, when Muriel Morse wrote of the need to acknowledge the impact of collective bargaining on merit systems. Morse advised that "... the decision is not where to draw the line [on collective bargaining]. The decision is about two kinds of personnel systems, and they have different concerns. We can no longer believe we can be half collective bargaining and half merit system."[7] But the manager of the 1980s knows that both premises have remained in place and still a third standard has been added since Morse expressed this concern. That new decision premise is equal employment opportunity.

The equal employment opportunity premise

The third premise managers are asked to adopt in managing people comes out of the equal employment opportunity movement. Actions in support of equal access are actions which diminish barriers to full participation for historically disadvantaged groups. These interests are advanced by those groups in the population which, by virtue of some racial, ethnic, gender, age, physical, or mental impairment, gain special legal protection against discrimination in the workplace. Their social interests are diverse in terms of the way each group has historically related to the employment situation. However, blacks, women, older citizens, and handicapped persons are all tied together by their experience of discrimination. The interest at stake in each case is to remove that discrimination which inhibits equality of access to positions in work organizations. . . .

In juxtaposing the EEO decision premise with the merit and collective negotiation premises, defining the problem of discrimination becomes central. If equal access requires only the observance of nondiscrimination, EEO poses no direct barrier to achieving goals advanced by the other decision premises. But if it prescribes positive action, EEO rapidly preempts the place of competing goals. Minorities and women today are advocating the institutionalization of positive action rather than simply nondiscrimination. Their reasoning is as follows: A nondiscrimination policy premised on the assumption that the problem is individual prejudice makes sense only under limiting conditions. Nondiscrimination is a reasonable approach to providing equal access in employment only if those who compete have an equal opportunity, controlling for natural ability, to acquire the characteristics that make one a likely choice for a position in the absence of active intentional discrimination. However, in the absence of equal opportunity to acquire the proper characteristics, positive measures must be taken, not only to ensure that subtle organizational practices are not limiting opportunity but also to break the cycle . . . of structural discrimination. Given the fact that intentional discrimination, though still present in many contemporary organizations, is only part of the problem, current approaches call for affirmative action programs (positive action) designed to change results. The thrust here is literally to place women and minorities into positions in which they have been historically underrepresented, rather than simply depend on the good intentions of nondiscrimination policies in competing for those positions. Theoretically, this would result in a change in organizational practices inhibiting access and contribute toward the breakdown of structural discrimination.

Competing claims and managerial response

. . . While Stephen Bailey may be right in his observation that ". . . the most essential courage in the public service is the courage to decide,"[8] responsible decisions in the competing claims area hinge on adopting a mode of analysis which highlights the impacts of alternatives on affected groups and provides a framework for allocating costs. In other words, managers need an ethical framework for human resource decision making, a device to empower them as ethical agents in competing claims decision making.

If . . . the manager is to be cast as a moral agent in these competing claim controversies, analytical tools are needed to reduce the pervasive ambiguity around issues of obligation, authority, and responsibility for personnel actions. The following ethical framework has been produced from extensive discussions of and reflections on a series of "ethical dilemma" cases written by government managers.[9] The framework aims to empower managers as ethical agents in competing claims decision making.

Ethical framework for human resource decision making

Specifically, the framework offered here does three things. It provides a way of identifying those interests that should be taken into account by managers; it provides analytical tools for assessing the relative degree of obligation each interest generates; and it invites reflection on issues of authority and responsibility in managerial decision making.

The first step is to identify those interests that must be taken into account in any competing claims situation. For this analysis we turn to what is called "stakeholder theory," a theory developed in an effort to incorporate the claims of broader publics into private sector management decision making.[10] Adapted to this analysis, stakeholders are individuals, groups, or classes whose lives are affected by management decisions. In other words, they are "parties at interest" in a particular decision context. An organization is dependent on and responsible to the stakeholders whose lives it affects. While no one group of stakeholders has total claim to what constitutes appropriate conduct for an organization, when management decisions impinge, stakeholders have a right to say they are injured. An organization must respond in a way that ensures that its activities don't harm those it affects—an obligation which binds despite the current state of regulation or deregulation. While this doesn't require acceding to every stakeholder demand, it does require that managers seek to understand stakeholder concerns and proposals arising out of a serious expectation of potential harm.

In seeking to understand stakeholder demands and management's obligations vis-à-vis those demands, a simple conceptual framework makes the distinction initially between negative and affirmative obligation and suggests that negative responsibilities are more stringent than affirmative responsibilities. The responsibility to avoid injury to others is a more stringent obligation than the responsibility to help others. In his writing on corporate ethics, Michael Rion uses a simple example to illustrate this point:

Suppose you encounter a beggar soliciting donations as you walk down the street of a large city. Should you make a contribution? Should you aid her to find shelter or even take a continuing interest in her welfare upon returning to your home town? The answers are not obvious, for they depend upon your understanding of why persons must beg, your charitable commitments and priorities, and your financial means. Judging affirmative responsibilities to do good to others can easily lead to disagreements about values and appropriate roles but if asked whether you should intentionally push the beggar off her chair into the rain puddle, surely all moral agents would say that you should not. Morally, we agree that we should not harm others.[11]

Customarily, ethics in public administration means the obligation to avoid injury. Avoiding injury is the principle behind the public's insistence that managers avoid waste and public deception. Our scheme for guiding managers in competing claims decision making focuses on such negative responsibilities. Obviously this does not restrict managers merely to avoiding and correcting injury. Some even argue that, in the last decades, the role definition of the public manager has expanded to include the pursuance of social justice. But this essay's analysis of competing claims is concerned with the avoidance of injury rather than a more expansive notion of "doing good."

No one disputes that the administrator bears a negative obligation to avoid injuring others in the execution of public service. But the nature of injury requires careful analysis. Take the case of a manager charged with drafting a Reduction in Force (RIF) policy for an agency. Assume the agency acknowledges the American Federation of State, County, and Municipal Employees (AFSCME) as the representative of the nonprofessional employees. The professional staff has, for the most part, been selected and promoted through a civil service system relying heavily on test scores and formal credentials. But in the last three years the total staff has gone from 2 percent to 20 percent representation of minorities in all positions; and women, always well represented in non-professional slots, have increased their presence in professional jobs from 2 percent four years ago to 18 percent today. These gains are due largely to an aggressive affirmative action program implemented by the agency.

In this situation the manager is challenged to understand the nature of harm involved in any particular RIF action and then balance that action against another potential harm inflicted by an alternative action. Clearly this case presents potential for injury on a number of fronts. In order to analyze the nature and extent of injury, the manager first asks who the potential "stakeholders" are in this dilemma. Again, stakeholders are the parties affected by a decision. Next, the manager asks what rights or interests each party has. Finally, the manager considers the nature of all the conflicting values among the stakeholders and rates the relative importance of each value. Doing harm to the interest of some stakeholders might derive from avoiding injury to other stakeholders. In this ethical dilemma the stakeholders would include at least the following:

1. Union AFSCME and union membership (nonprofessional)
2. Professional staff selected and promoted through the merit system
3. New women professional staff
4. New minority employees, professional and nonprofessional
5. Agency beneficiaries/clients
6. Agency head
7. Administrator reporting the dilemma

Each of these parties could be injured by the administrator's response. Avoiding injury to every party is not possible in this case. Typically, this kind of ambiguity dominates decision making in the public sector. But the task of the administrator is to sort out these potential injuries, and within his or her authority, to select the least injurious decision from the value rankings derived from thoughtful analysis. Viewed from this perspective, though the most stringent obligation of the administrator is to avoid doing harm, defining this obligation in a particular context admittedly is difficult.

In this sorting and shifting process, managers are guided by their own ethical systems. Ethicists describe such systems as ". . . an ordered set of moral standards and rules of conduct by reference to which, with the addition of factual knowledge one can determine in any situation of choice what a person ought or ought not to do. . . ."[12] Two distinctively different ethical systems give rise to two ethical standards which guide action. The first system, deontological ethics, asserts that certain features of acts render them good or bad irrespective of consequence. Classic examples of good acts are keeping promises and telling the truth. We ought to always tell the truth, and to keep agreements, because of the value inherent in the acts—in other words, because it is right. The second ethical system, utilitarian ethics, sees an act as right if it produces a greater balance of good over evil. In this second system, the moral quality of actions is dependent on what they bring about or try to bring about.[13] If the consequences are "good," then the act is right.

Most managers are neither pure deontologists nor pure utilitarians, but rather operate according to a kind of ethical pluralism. Guided by this synthesis of moral systems, managers typically might conclude that the moral reason for or against some action resides in its consequences, while the rationale for or against other actions stems from their being of a kind required or prohibited by duty. When acting out of ethical pluralism, managers need to develop a capacity for sensitive moral judgment, for often one must apply both sorts of moral reasoning to the same actions. It might be that the consequences of some action would be so bad that it should not be undertaken even though one has a *prima facie* obligation to do it.

Taking the RIF example above, clearly one has an obligation to keep the long-standing commitment made to the union to lay off employees according to seniority; and in the absence of moral reasons against it, seniority would be the prime determinant of RIF decision making. But, in this particular context, the consequence of such a decision-making rule would be to lay off 90 percent of the minority nonprofessional employees in the organization and only 2 percent of their white co-workers. The consequences of following the seniority decision rule are so bad in terms of adverse impact on minority employees that a manager may reject the seniority criterion notwithstanding the long-standing commitment to the union to follow it.

The assumption of this essay up to this point has been that the manager or the organization has been sufficiently involved in the injurious act to trigger an obligation to cease the injury or to compensate. But often in organizations, particularly in instances of competing claims, the whole issue of responsibility to act is problematic. In many real-life situations, before managers even get to the "what is right?" issues, they want to know when it is even appropriate to exercise their own moral judgment. Clearly if they are personally involved in causing the injury, moral judgment is called for, as illustrated in the RIF policy-making discussion above. But sometimes managers are also obliged to correct injury caused by others.

The conditions triggering obligatory action are enumerated in an ethical decision rule called the "Kew Gardens Principle," a label borrowed from the widely publicized murder in the Kew Gardens section of New York City, witnessed by 30 to 40 silent bystanders. The principle suggests action is obligatory to the extent that the following conditions prevail:

1. *Need.* There is a clear need for aid. . . .
2. *Proximity.* The agent is "close" to the situation, not necessarily in space but certainly in terms of notice; . . .
3. *Capability.* The agent has some means by which to aid the one in need without undue risk to the agent . . .
4. *Last resort.* No one else is likely to help. . . .[14]

In reflecting back on the RIF example, assume that the individual manager is not responsible for drafting the RIF policy, but simply for implementing it. Hence, there is no specific injury implicated by implementation action. However, if a manager is in a position to make a more accurate assessment of the injury suffered by certain stakeholders as the result of a RIF and to feed that information into the construction of an organization-wide policy, the character of obligation may change. Take this example:

Assume you are a division head directing an engineering division in an agency about to undergo a 30 percent RIF. The RIF policy developed by the staff of the agency head has determined to cut positions in the professional ranks beginning with the lowest civil service positions first. The historically all white engineering division has diversified in recent years, through the efforts of a highly committed personnel unit. The division has been able to recruit and maintain minority engineers so that the division's engineering workforce is 10 percent minority. Because the minority engineers joined the unit in entry level positions, they are currently concentrated in the lowest third of the civil service grades. The chief of the personnel unit in the department has just been replaced and the new chief clearly does not share the commitment to minority recruitment and retention. Because of the more relaxed EEO regulatory environment, generally you believe there is little sentiment in the organization as a whole for continuing to press EEO issues. You are sure that implementing the policy of achieving the reduction by eliminating the lower grade positions is tantamount to RIFing all of the minority engineers.

The question is: does this manager have an obligation to try to reshape the policy or at least secure an exemption in his unit? The Kew Gardens Principle suggests that an obligation might exist. The minority group employees have been injured by a discriminatory policy in the past and through a nonconsciously discriminatory policy are now about to lose their jobs (need). The manager in this case is close enough to the situation to have the vital information about the impact of a position-based RIF (proximity). Whether or not he or she could act without jeopardizing his or her job or future effectiveness in the organization is uncertain (capability). It does appear that the manager in this case may be the only one who can come to the aid of the minority engineers (last resort).

To sum up this presentation of an ethical framework for human resource decision making, the basic moral principle counsels managers to avoid hurting others. Sensitive ethical analysis is required to actually define an injury in terms of all stakeholders involved and to weigh injuries caused by a particular action. But even managers who avoid doing injury to others may be further obligated to correct or prevent injury caused by others, according to the Kew Gardens Principle. This principle offers a blueprint for those areas where there is a less stringent obligation than in the requirement to avoid injury, but a more stringent obligation than the affirmative obligation to do good.

Conclusion

In the late 1970s Warren Bennis described the expression of competing interests in organizations as "the politics of multiple advocacies—vocal, demanding, often 'out of sync' with each other."[15] Bennis spoke for many public sector executives when he described his organization as analogous to an anvil on which a fragmented society hammers. Today the society remains fragmented and groups still hammer, though the force of their blows may be lightened by deregulation. This article argues for moving beyond the anvil imagery of the analogy.

The image and fact of paralyzed managers, able only to reflect imprints of competing interests, must change. Change will come from a more self-conscious definition of the human resource manager as a morally responsible actor. The challenge for the public sector manager is to move beyond lamenting the expression of strong group interests and toward responding sensitively and fairly to expressions of hurt. We do not claim to tell managers how to weigh different expressions of hurt. Moral reasoning may lead individual managers to give primacy to different decision premises in similar cases. Still, whatever social interest is served by a particular decision, this article presents ethical reflection as a mode of response which rejects the imagery of the human resource manager as a passive actor, buffeted to and fro on a sea of competing claims and imprisoned in a role devoid of conscience. The manager as a self-consciously ethical decision maker is an active listener who sensitively and thoroughly considers the competing interests at stake, exercises informed moral judgment regarding the balance of these interests, and purposefully adopts the decision premises guiding action.

Notes

1. The term "decision premise" is taken from Herbert Simon's classic work, *Administrative Behavior*, 2nd ed. (New York: Free Press, 1965). It suggests a starting point for decision making which accepts as "given" both goals or values to be achieved and a specified set of alternative strategies for achieving those goals.

2. Herbert Kaufman, "Administrative Decentralization and Political Power," *Public Administration Review* 29 (January/February 1969), 3.

3. M. Chandler, *Management Rights and Union Interests* (New York: McGraw Hill, 1964), 64; *The Public Interest in Government Labor Relations* (Cambridge, Mass.: Ballinger Publishing Co., 1977), 19.

4. Wilbur C. Rich, *The Politics of Urban Personnel Policy: Reformers, Politicians, and Bureaucrats* (Port Washington, N.Y.: Kennikat Press, 1982), 25.

5. O. Glenn Stahl, *Public Personnel Administration*, 6th ed. (New York: Harper and Row, 1971), 41.

6. Frederick C. Mosher, *Democracy and the Public Service*, 2nd ed. (New York: Oxford University Press, 1968), 203–204.

7. Muriel M. Morse, "Shall We Bargain Away the Merit System?" *Public Personnel Review* 24 (October 1963), 239–243.

8. Stephen K. Bailey, "Ethics and the Public Service" in R. C. Martin (ed.), *Public Administration and Democracy* (Syracuse: Syracuse University Press, 1965), 296.

9. Valid scholarship in management ethics must be closely linked to moral quandaries as they are experienced by managers. This analysis has grown from discussions with government executives participating in the North Carolina Government Executive Institute (GEI). The GEI is an executive development program available to state, local and some federal executives. (For GEI purposes executives are defined as managers of managers.) In preparation for our management ethics session I ask participants to

complete a management ethics case writing assignment. The core of the case assignment reads:

Reflect back to a situation where you experienced an ethical dilemma arising from a conflict between action dictated by your own personal code of ethics and that expected by the formal or informal norms of your agency or the public you serve. Describe the dilemma in one paragraph, changing names (if used) and/or department so as to protect your anonymity and that of others involved.

Of the 150 executives participating in the GEI over the past two years, 45 have chosen to submit ethics cases for class discussion. About half of these cases dealt with human resource management issues and centered on competing claims pressed on the manager. The ethical framework presented is a product of (1) my understanding of the decision premise advocated by competing interests in our society, (2) discussion and reflection on the experiences of managers at the point where divergent interests converge and jointly press for primacy, (3) application of ethical theory to these cases.

10. For a discussion of stakeholder theory application see Henry B. Schacht and Charles W. Powers, "Business Responsibility and the Public Policy Process" in Thornton Bradshaw and David Vogel (eds.), *Corporations and Their Critics* (New York: McGraw Hill, 1981), 25–32.

11. Michael Rion, "Ethical Principles" (Columbus, Indiana, 1980) (mimeographed).

12. Paul Taylor, *Principles of Ethics,* (Dickenson Publishing Company, 1975), 12.

13. William K. Frankena, *Ethics,* 2nd ed. (Englewood Cliffs, N.J.: Prentice-Hall, 1973), 23

14. John G. Simons, Charles W. Powers, Jon P. Gunneman, *The Ethical Investor* (New Haven: Yale University Press, 1972), 22–25.

15. Warren Bennis, "Where Have All the Leaders Gone?" *Technology Review* (March/April 1977), 39.

Hard Choices: Justifying Bureaucratic Decisions

———————————————— Douglas T. Yates, Jr.

Questions of value and ethics hang over most public policy discussions like a cloud—or perhaps a thin vapor. We know the questions are critical and ubiquitous, but we typically have trouble setting our hands on them. . . .

Before establishing my arbitrary boundaries and setting out my approach to value conflict, let me say a word or two more about the fundamental value problem as I see it. Unless we specify what kinds of officials, policies, and value problems we are interested in, we might include virtually every imaginable aspect of political life and behavior. . . .

I want to pick out one corner of the map of officials, policies, and value conflicts that has been given much attention in an older literature but not recently. The area I have in mind concerns the role of appointive officials and bureaucrats as makers of public policy in a democratic society. I assume that they have some discretion both in designing the policy and in choosing the process by which the decision will be made. Moreover, I think significant values are at stake in both kinds of choices. I pick the value-choosing role of bureaucrats for three reasons: (1) it is commonly agreed that public policy is increasingly made by administrators, at the stages of both policy formulation and implementation; (2) emphasis on bureaucrats permits me to duck the debate about what constitutes proper representative behavior (when this depends on the choice of one or another broader democratic theory); and (3) in almost any democratic theory you choose, the choicemaking, "valuemaking" aspects of bureaucratic behavior is highly problematic. Whether policy and administration are separable or connected, it does seem odd in a democratic regime to give appointive officials a major role in value choices. It is not merely a matter of who guards the guardians—certainly a time-honored question—but more precisely, who regulates or controls the bureaucratic policymakers' values and how. I believe bureaucrats also play a further *critical* role in the realm of values to the extent that they set and administer the processes by which policy disputes are raised, argued out, heard, and disposed of in the decisionmaking process.

To avoid another long-standing empirical debate about the extent of bureaucratic independence and discretion (from statute or whatever), let me simply assert that bureaucrats are in the business of choosing and balancing values routinely—at least whenever they propose policy or interpret statutes. I can imagine someone replying that there are real constraints on the bureaucrat's ability to choose freely among different values. I cannot imagine anyone saying that the bureaucrat's role in value choice and balancing is a trivial feature of American government.

My first premise then, which is of particular interest and concern in a democracy, is that bureaucrats have a major role in making value choices and establishing processes by which competing values are dealt with in public decisions. Of course, if most public policy decisions turned out to contain only minor value trade-offs for the bureaucrat to worry about, my first premise might be correct but also quite uninteresting. In fact, in certain writings on bureaucracy and administration, the doctrine is advanced that decisions rest (or should rest) on criteria of efficiency and effectiveness (which criteria most reasonable people could agree upon and about which there is arguably only an interesting problem in terms of adequate measurement). Woodrow Wilson argued such a position and Robert McNamara may be understood, if slightly caricatured, to seek the same kind of value neutrality in dispassionate systems analysis, cost-benefit analysis, and the like. In this respect, it would be difficult to argue as a matter of principle that the government should receive less bang for the buck. . . . I believe that there are some policy issues for which this kind of value neutrality, given the name of efficiency, probably obtains or is nearly approximated. But I believe that such policy issues are rare, a minority of public decisions.

Consider the current inventory of pressing public policy issues. These issues include affirmative action, busing, environmental protection, welfare reform, abortion, health insurance, energy policy, and energy "taxes," to name just a few. Now the heroic systems analyst might want to say that, analyzed carefully enough, these are really questions of benefit and cost and that different policies can be settled on efficiency or effectiveness grounds. However, on careful inspection, it turns out that this analytical heroism is at least incomplete and perhaps misguided. Taking any of the issues listed above, it seems plain that the public debate is, in the final analysis, concerned with the application of major public values, however understood, such as liberty, equality, justice, community. To take one example, busing can be construed as a strategy for increasing educational performance on average. But it is hard to avoid the conclusion that in a fundamental way, blacks are making equality claims and whites are making liberty claims (that is, freedom to maintain their neighborhoods); and the government may be seeking to alter existing notions of community.

So the first point is that the daily life of bureaucrats involves the identification and balancing of major public values. If these values were reasonably defined, it might be relatively easy for a bureaucrat to construct—implicitly or explicitly—a value impact analysis for a given policy and to specify relevant trade-offs.

Indeed, I think the first obligation of the appointive official or bureaucrat is to be *explicit* about the value premises and implications of public decisions. The reason for this goes back to the difference between legislators and bureaucrats mentioned above. We might exempt legislators from this value-accounting on the pluralist grounds that they are responding to constituent interests and that this response is considered a legitimate, indeed essential, way to justify value positions in a democratic society. Bureaucrats lack this justification of their policy decisions, and this is why their attention to providing a value analysis is of particular significance. If bureaucrats are going to make value choices, they should inform the rest of us value-laden voters and consumers of policies what the operative values behind public decisions are and how they conflict (when they do).

This value clarification is especially important where policy decision involves policy conflicts and trade-offs. It is there, most especially, that we citizens might want to know why the government is doing X rather than Y. (Obviously too, I believe that many interesting policy decisions will elicit and sustain a subtle analysis of value conflicts as they exist in different policy options.) Thus, if the first question of public policy is "What should government do?" any adequate answer should include a self-conscious assessment of the implications of policy for major public values such as liberty, equality, community, or the public interest.

This much may seem entirely unobjectionable. And we might suspect that given more time, bureaucrats could easily do value impact statements along with their myriad other analyses. In this halcyon world of philosopher-kings—Washington style—a new cover memo would emerge from officials which would comment on equality-efficiency trade-offs, liberty-equality trade-offs, and the like.

We might be happy to achieve this much if we believed the resulting discourse on values would offer clearer choices, illuminate policy dilemmas, and otherwise inform. Unhappily, we know all too well that the language of values is at present insufficiently precise to support impact statements that compare with those of economists, scientists, and other such experts.

I do not wish to delve into the substantive meaning of those timeless public values. I would offer instead a more modest approach to value clarification which will, I hope, add some additional criteria of assessment to debates about the ideas of liberty and equality themselves. I can make this point most clearly by using the example of equality arguments.

Equality claims

Most public officials would agree that equality has become a dominant idea in modern political discourse. Just think how many policy debates involve an equality claim on one side or the other. In a large number of policy disputes, we will find some equality claim in a strong if not ascendant position; and in a large number of policy disputes, we will find an equality claim in direct conflict with another equality claim. What are we to make of this? At first glance, it would seem that any hoped-for "value impact statement" has suffered a severe blow. For if it is hard enough to identify and trade off claims of liberty versus equality, for example, how in the world are we to assess conflicts between different equality claims as they arise in a particular policy dispute?

There is one other reason why equality is such an important but slippery principle. Many discussions about liberty, justice, rights of various sorts, and fairness revolve around the question of equality— that is, the "issue" can often be restated in terms of equal liberties, rights, and so forth. The idea of right seems to include an idea of equality.

However, the lamentable fact is that the concept of equality, in most of its formulations, is nearly empty. The simple equation $X = Y$ says very little without a great deal of further specification of what is being distributed in what amounts to whom and by what criteria. Perhaps the best way to write the basic equality statement is $? = ?$, so as to make the point that invoking the equal sign accomplishes precious little in the way of normative argument. We still have to figure out *who* is to receive equal shares and *what* is to be equalized.

It is possible to construct a basic grammar that highlights many of the persistent points of dispute in discussions of a principle like equality. On the *who* side, it is necessary to make clear in the first place whether we are talking about individuals or collectives (such as a state or nation). If the former, is each individual to count discretely as one (unitary equality) or as part of some imagined class of people (for example, blacks, women, patients requiring kidney dialysis?) If the latter, how do we count or compare classes of people? Are we concerned about equality within groups (equal access to dialysis for all kidney patients) or equality between groups (that is, aggregate equality relationships between blacks and whites)?

So far this logic is indeed simple; and it would not be hard for a public official to make clear what accounting method he or she is using. However, there are also some interesting complexities here that are harder to disentangle. For example, how do you decide whom to include in the relevant catchment area when adding up individual interest for the purpose of equalizing treatment? In the *Bakke* or *DeFunis* cases, concerning affirmative action policies, is the relevant catchment area the state of Washington or California or the nation as a whole? In thinking about equal claims to access to unspoiled wilderness in Alaska or the High Sierras, do you include the resident of New Jersey as well as citizens more immediately affected by Storm King or the Alaska Pipeline? The question is: Who has *standing* in the legal sense and how do we think about this question when residents of New York or New Jersey increasingly claim an interest in what happens to wildlife in Alaska or wilderness in California?

A second problem that the public official must increasingly think about is how to balance individual interests against corporate (in the broadest sense) and institutional interests. In this respect, what sense do we make of a claim of a group of urban residents who say they constitute a community or neighborhood and that the interests of that neighborhood should be treated equally (one-to-one) with other "neighborhoods." (This counting problem is, of course, familiar to all of us in the Virginia Compromise with the apportionment of votes to individuals in the House and to collectivities in the Senate.) My point is that increasingly we are faced with groups of individuals purporting to be indivisible, organic collectivities (more radical elements of the woman's movement and the Quebec "nationalists" come to mind), and unless we can figure out how to count interests (holding individuals equal or equalizing treatment of collectivities), any major problem of distribution is likely to be muddled. Put another way, until we can figure out this counting problem, we will have a hard time knowing whether we are making policy for individuals, say a truck driver; interest groups, say the Teamsters; or collectivities, say labor. Needless to say, the more public officials are asked to balance the interests of collectivities—business, labor, the frostbelt, neighborhoods, the young, the black community—the more difficult their task of calculation becomes. In the extreme case, the only logical result is corporatism, one vote or share for each entity. More frequently, the effort to equalize treatment of these groups leads to Theodore Lowi's interest group pluralism, where one group after another is accommodated by government. In the end, however, it is hard to know whether there is more or less equality as a result.

On the *what* side of equality arguments, there is a need to specify what the value is that is being distributed—money, opportunity, and so on. Then there is a need to make clear what further factors enter into the distribution—for example, need or merit of some sort. Finally, there is usually a need to specify the benchmark according to which equal distribution is measured. In the simplest case, if group X is way behind historically in its share of a value, does equality require an immediate equal result, a proportional increase, or merely an equal opportunity to catch up? This is essentially the problem of starting-line versus finish-line fairness related to the question of specifying the historical point at which the race began. My guess is that it is impossible to appraise the claims made by "disadvantaged" groups as well as "backlash" groups without specifying something about the historical benchmark to be used in making comparisons over time.

I have given this brief account of the simple grammar implicit in equality claims because I believe that although some of the terms may seem abstract, they are in fact pivotal issues in ordinary public decisions.[1] I do not expect public officials to torture themselves over all the nuances of normative argument. But they do have an obligation to attempt an explicit accounting of how they are applying the values and principles they seek to endorse.

A first summary

So far I have attempted to make the following arguments about value discourse in public policymaking.

1. Bureaucrats must choose between and implement values to a significant extent. They also play a major role in designing and implementing the processes by which value-laden decisions are made.
2. In most but not all policy disputes, there are significant conflicts and trade-offs between values.
3. As an example, we have seen that many policy disputes involve conflicting equality claims.
4. Public officials cannot resolve value conflicts in any philosophical sense, but they can identify relevant values and the conflict they enter into.
5. Moreover, public officials can and should make clear what language, what words, they are using in treating values.

6. Further, as we saw in the case of equality, value discourse can be expressed in relatively simple terms that reveal not only what public officials are talking about, but also how they are doing their accounting—how they are counting heads and allocations.

From these points, I wish to draw one central conclusion that speaks to the problem of reconciling bureaucratic discretion and power with democratic norms. I believe the public official's fundamental moral obligation in a democracy is to pay increased attention to the definition and treatment of values the more these values are in conflict in a decision and the more difficulty there is in doing the accounting of who gets what. In the simple case where, for example, there is a clear and dominant equality principle at stake, and little problem in accounting, the public official may owe us as citizens no more than a terse statement of the justification for the public decision. But in more complex cases, where the value conflicts are great and the accounting problems are substantial, I believe public officials should provide a more thorough value analysis as one of the central justifications of public decision. Indeed, this is how I would define responsibility in bureaucratic decisionmaking. Without such an accounting, citizens can never know how and why their officials decided to act as they did. Without that knowledge, it is hard to see how the idea of democratic control of administration can be anything more than a dangerous fiction.

One public official who has made an attempt to perform explicit value analysis is former Secretary of Transportation William Coleman at the time of his decision on whether Concorde could land at Kennedy airport. In his written decision, Coleman performed a careful cost-benefit analysis that involved an explicit concern for legal, environmental, and political values. In short, Coleman sought to give the interested parties and the public a full accounting of his thought processes and of his own weighing of relevant values. As he wrote in his decision,

This decision involves environmental, technological, and international considerations that are as complex as they are controversial, and do not lend themselves to easy or graceful evaluation, let alone comparison. I shall nonetheless attempt in some detail to explain my evaluation of the most significant issues—those raised in the EIS, by the proponents and opponents of the Concorde at the January 5 public hearing, and in the submissions to the docket—and the reasons I have decided as I have. For I firmly believe that public servants have the duty to express in writing their reasons for taking major actions, so that the public can judge the fairness and objectivity of such action. Moreover, explaining our reasons in writing may help us avoid unreasonable actions. A decision that "cannot be explained" is very likely to be an arbitrary decision.[2]

The strength of Coleman's analysis is that his concern to spell out value considerations both enabled citizens to better understand the Concorde problem and, equally important, gave the citizen an opportunity to see what kind of person, with what kind of concerns and values, was making decisions in the office of the Secretary of Transportation.

Another fundamental reason the value-choosing role of bureaucrats is a critical aspect of policymaking in the American democratic system is that we increasingly lack any clear or coherent justification (or set of justifications) for government intervention in our society. There have, of course, been such doctrines in the past which at least appeared to be well understood if not always perfectly clear. In a much simpler world, those who advocated the view that the "government which governs least governs best" did at least have a decision rule that provided a guide to action. When in doubt, don't intervene. Keep government out. More recently, the New Deal faith in government as a potent instrument for solving critical social and economic problems also provided a kind of decision rule. The test was to identify "critical" problems and then explain why they deserved this definition. Of course, given an enthusiastic and adventurous government, the New Deal test for public intervention and action did not provide a clear or particularly stringent decision rule.

The most rigorous criteria for justifying public intervention are probably those of economic theory, but even here we have considerable difficulty sustaining any persuasive tests of appropriate government intervention. Modern economic theory contemplates a market mechanism that should be allowed to function unless certain market failures or other special conditions arise. Concepts of market failure, externalities, merit goods, and public goods are offered as exceptions to a general rule that the market should be allowed to operate "freely"—or at least within constraints imposed by antitrust policy, truthful advertising, and the like. Curiously, however, the exceptions to the market "ideal" have, in my view as a noneconomist, become the exceptions that very often disprove the rule. Put another way, in a complicated, intertwined economy, with a large public sector to begin with, it is easy for an alert economist to find market failures, externalities, and public goods in many different places.

If we cannot find justification for public action in a firmly rooted public philosophy, like "the government which governs least," or an economic theory, in earlier incarnations, what restraints or normative principles exist at all to suggest that government should *not* act on a particular policy problem? My answer is that in our present governmental climate, there are almost no such restraints or systematic principles. This means that a kind of "open season" exists for government, and indeed we have by now become used to a familiar pattern: if government finds a new problem like drug addition or energy conservation or environmental protection, it will create a bureaucracy and throw a new program at it.

If this analysis is anywhere near correct, it strongly reinforces my central argument that bureaucratic policymakers are often deciding when, why, and how to act and are making substantial value choices for specific policy arenas, and in addition, are implicitly fashioning new rationales and precedents for government intervention. If this is true, it only reinforces my argument that bureaucratic policymakers owe citizens in a democracy a careful accounting of the reasons why they have decided to act, what public purposes they are pursuing, and what values they have emphasized as against reasonable alternatives. In addition, this accounting should both bolster the legitimacy of governmental action in given choice situations and strengthen the citizen's ability to comprehend the general role of governments.

Notes

1. A dissection of different notions of equality has recently been attempted by a number of us working at Yale. See Douglas Rae and others, *Equalities* (Cambridge, Mass.: Harvard University Press, 1981).

2. Department of Transportation, The Secretary's Decision on Concorde Supersonic Transport, Washington, D.C., February 4, 1976, p. 7.

Professional
Ethics

Frank P. Sherwood

Professional codes of ethics do not seem to be a very effective means of inducing the type of behavior we desire in our public officeholders. A major share of the Watergate culprits were lawyers. Next to physicians, they perhaps have the most specific set of professional requirements for behavior. Yet, the evidence seems clear that the norms and traditions of the legal profession had little bearing on Watergate actors' decisions and actions, including those of the President of the United States.

There are probably a good many reasons why codes have relatively limited usefulness. Two come immediately to mind. The first is that we live in many different worlds, playing segmented roles. Each has its code of behavior, formal or informal. The demands on the politician are different from those on the lawyer; and, when you put the demands of both roles on the same individual, dilemmas are inevitably created. Thus, the real issue is what values one brings to the choice among codes.

Secondly, codes tend to be universalistic; they set outer boundaries for behavior. They prescribe the limits of transgression. In a sense, the codes take a *Thou shalt not...* stance, whereas many of our moral problems occur in choices where limits are seen only dimly, if at all.

Watergate can be described as an extreme case of a problem facing every public leader—how to behave in such a way as to honor the nation's democratic imperatives and at the same time effectively perform its important public business.

It is easy to underestimate the energy and effort required to

Reprinted by permission from *Public Management* magazine (June 1975): 13–14.

face one's own value system and then to relate that to consciously personal decisions and behavior patterns.

We must realize how complex is the environment in which each public leader functions. City managers probably realize that more than most; a scant 30 years ago the systematic repair of potholes seemed like *the* urban problem. Coincident with complexity has come high interest articulation. That is, the forces that operate on the public leader are increasingly coherent, organized; they demand from him allocations and behaviors that are consistent with the values they hold. It's easy to be overwhelmed by the plethora of environmental forces, some of which are obviously better organized than others.

And, sense of defeat—or frustration—can lead to over-simplification. It can mean selecting out certain elements in the environment as having legitimacy, an exercise which is typically influenced by the degree to which values are shared. We like best the people who think the way we do. That such oversimplification can lead to great trouble will surprise no one, but I think it is far less understood that the fear of challenge to one's personal values is frequently the springboard for such over-simplification.

While all leaders face the requirement to deal with their environments as fully as possible, the public leader has a special kind of responsibility. In essence, his most fundamental obligation is to protect and support the democratic process. Conflict and divergence of view are at the heart of the process; and, debates and delayed policy-making do not necessarily conform to the norms of orderly administrative process.

My experience is that many administrators have great difficulty relating their democratic commitment to their day-to-day activity. Though they are democratic in their ideology, their need for achievement and high task-orientation make them very skeptical of any process that accepts amateurism, is indulgent toward delay, and which may threaten the quality of the ultimate decision. It is not at all unusual to find public leaders who will proclaim the virtues of democracy at the voting and legislative level, but practice the most outrageous authoritarianism in the management of their own organizations.

In effect, the distinction between the public and the private leader is based largely on the degree of primacy given to the nurturing and support of the democratic process. That support comes in many ways, of course, but it all adds up to the holding of a public interest value. While we should expect *all* public-officeholders to honor the public interest, it is a particular demand that a professional careerist must make on himself. . . .

City managers have special problems relating to the democratic ethic. The grass roots, for all its beauty, can be insensitive, frustrating, and just plain tiring. More than that, it can be uncaring and unappreciative. In studies of the utilization of time by managers, I have been impressed by the conflict they experience between support for the process (open door) and task accomplishment (efficiency and effectiveness).

Many early city managers had little patience with democracy. They ran things; and, people were so happy finally to get some services and improvements that they accepted the dictatorial style. While there are many conditions in our cities that cause us to yearn for those old domineering types, I believe we are also more prizing of our democratic system and more aware today of intrusions on it. There is no way to return to times when demands were vastly more simplified.

While it is easy to identify ways in which the world of the urban manager has changed and therefore posed new value dilemmas, it is clearly another matter to be specific about means of coping more consciously with the problem. . . .

Higher standards lie not so much in demands for behavior (which tends to be a characteristic of codes) as in organizational and societal processes that insist the individual consciously confront his values and take responsibility for consequent behavior. Specifically, we must build the value dimension into our daily thinking, working, and acting in organizational life.

The following three questions may help to put some flesh on what may yet appear to be a fairly indistinct skeleton.

1. *To what extent do you consciously consider the value premises of your recommendations, decisions, and action?* (If you accept Herbert Simon's general theory, *every* decision has a value element.)

2. *To what extent have value assumptions been an articulated part of the policy development dialogue with legislators, citizens, and subordinates?* (One budget officer said he was *surprised* to find, in a classroom exercise, the degree to which his personal values influenced his position on tax policy.)

3. *To what extent have you accepted the definition of public interest values as a desirable and needed dimension of training and development for yourself and others?* (In most professional graduate education programs in public administration, courses in values are fairly hard to find and relatively unpopulated. They are virtually nonexistent in the menu of training courses.)

If it is true that the urban manager is relatively unprogrammed and somewhat free to use himself as he sees best, then it appears hardly arguable that he be given a good deal more help in making the choices inherent in such opportunities. And, the top manager has the further responsibility to construct organizational processes that help both administrators and legislators become more aware of what they stand for. Such efforts may just be our best and most practical means of combating big and little Watergates in the future.

PART 3

Managing Organizational Ethics

The Thinking Manager's Toolbox

Mark Pastin

It is better to know some of the questions than all of the answers.
—*James Thurber*

The purpose of this article is to provide a guide or toolbox for the thinking manager. It reviews the concepts, models, and some of the cases to provide a framework for asking questions that will enable you to probe the ethical reality of your firm and its environment, to find ethics edges, and to convert them into business advantages. In short, I offer a guide to using ethics both to explode unworkable assumptions that constrain thinking in your firm and to replace them with more adaptive assumptions and a more adaptive attitude toward assumptions.

The ground rules

We start with ground rules, the foundation of ethics. It is impossible to determine an organization's or a person's ethics unless we know the ground rules they play by. . . .

The fundamental definition for understanding ethics is: The ethics of a person or organization is the set of ground rules by which that person or organization acts.

In truth, even though all of us offer complex explanations of what we do and why, we act from a few simple principles. These principles are called ground rules. Once you have considered your options and reached a decision, that decision reflects the values you attach to different outcomes and what you are willing and not will-

Adapted from Mark Pastin, *The Hard Problems of Management: Gaining the Ethics Edge* (San Francisco: Jossey-Bass Inc., Publishers, 1986). Copyright © 1986 by Jossey-Bass Inc., 350 Sansome Street, San Francisco, CA 94104-1310. Reprinted with permission.

ing to do to obtain the outcomes. The same reasoning applies to organizations.

Thinking managers ask what their ground rules are. They also question the ground rules of their co-workers and of the organization itself. Exploring ground rules is uncomfortable, especially since those ground rules which we publicly endorse and those by which we act may be worlds apart. But exploring ground rules is more comfortable than being stuck in a situation in which your ground rules and the ground rules of your co-workers or organization do not mesh. You will be banging your head against the proverbial stone wall. The only thing good about banging your head against a stone wall is that it feels good when you stop....

Without a clear sense of your own ethics, you cannot develop a clear understanding of how to view your ethics in relation to the ethics of others and the organization. Once you understand what you view as ethical, you can begin to evaluate the ethics of your colleagues, your organization, and other organizations. To understand the ethics of colleagues and organizations, you need to be as hard-nosed as you are when you read the numbers and assess the competition.

The key to learning the ethics of individuals or organizations is simple: *Do not listen to what they say about ethics. Observe what they do.*

Thus, while a Techtron division advertises its commitment to affirmative action, the all-white all-male management group reveals its true ground rules. And while David Farnswarth tells his employees to develop bold ideas to carry D. F. Venture into new areas, any employee who develops one ends up on the pavement. The flip side to this is that many managers brag about how unethical they are as a way to build their image as rugged jungle fighters. But if you observe them, you will discover that some managers only say this because they think it is expected. Your opportunity may lie in being the only member of the firm who does not demand this tribal ritual.

Knowing your ground rules and the organization's ground rules is important to your career. Do your ethics, as determined by your ground rules, mesh with your organization's ground rules? If they do not, expect frustration and stagnation in a position you would like to move out of. This idea was reinforced through the example of women executives and how their attempts to move into line management positions are blocked by unwritten organizational ground rules ("It's every man for himself—literally!") enforced by a male-dominated management structure....

The thinking manager is not satisfied only to assess ground rules in the immediate business environment. The thinking manager also probes the disagreements between the ground rules of the business environment and the ground rules of other constituencies in society at large. He or she asks, "Where are there fundamental disagreements between local ground rules and those of outside constituencies?" This enables the thinking manager to foresee the directions from which ethical attacks and tragedies may come.

Nor is the thinking manager satisfied only to uncover the current ground rules of the firm, its environment, and society at large. He or she also probes ground rules to see where fundamental changes in ground rules are being negotiated in the form of ethical discussion. These are areas in which the basic conditions of doing business may shift (such as doing business in Iran) or slowly (such as paying more attention to the quality of the environment). Such areas are sources of grave threats and bold opportunities. One such area includes changes in ground rules compelled by changes in technologies. Probing ground rules for instability and change enables the thinking manager to determine the sources and directions of changes, rather than waiting to be run over by them.

Passing the ethics buck

If a manager finds an ethics gap between himself and his organization or between the organization and external constituencies, it is easy to ignore it, hoping it will go away. This attitude is pervasive in business and accounts for many of the problems business now faces.

Passing the ethics buck, hoping the problem will fade away, or slapping a Band-Aid on what requires major surgery are ways of ducking responsibility. Ethics Band-Aids are responsible for the Foreign Corrupt Practices Act, the Excess (unethical) Profits Tax, the regulatory stranglehold being applied to biotechnology, and the puzzling array of management techniques inflicted on organizations. Without true responsibility, there is only ethical retreat.

It is a sad truism that we do not act as ethically as we would like because "The company won't let us" or "I would if they would" or "That's business."... There is precedent for the unintended development of a situation in which irresponsible conduct is inevitable; it is the historical problem of the commons. To illustrate this problem, I use the example of the herdsman and a common pasture. The common pasture was eventually destroyed because everyone rationally tried to get his own "fair share" without considering the devastating overall effect on the pasture.

The commons problem shows most clearly in business in budget processes. So many people are striving for their fair piece of the pie that they fail to realize that it is impossible to eat an empty pie tin. And if everyone is concerned only with his or her fair share, someone ends up trying to survive on an empty tin.... You cannot avert a commons problem unless you recognize it *before* it comes to define organizational reality and undercut responsible action by entrenching the ground rule "You've got to get yours first." Commons are self-perpetuating responsibility solvents.

The issue of the commons is critical today because we are predisposed to regard information as a commons. It is generally believed that there is a right to know. This supposed right says that, other things being equal, everyone is equally entitled to use any piece of information. Just as the right to graze competes with the property rights of responsible herdsmen, so the right to know competes with the privacy rights of responsible individuals. As products increase in informational content and decrease in material content, the supposed right to know competes with the right of information creators to the fruits of their efforts.

The thinking manager asks of supposed rights: "If group A claims this right, then which group B is responsible for satisfying group A's claims? What is the overall impact of allowing this claimed right to become accepted as an actual right? Does this supposed right create a new commons?" Thinking managers ask these questions not because they are opposed to rights, but because they are opposed to rights claimed at the expense of others and at the expense of turning ever more resources into depletable commons.

The most important lesson of the commons is to recognize when commons problems undermine responsibility in your organization. Start by asking some key questions. Ask what commons problems affect your organization. Once you have identified the budget, common staff, space, nonbudgeted office supplies, and the other obvious commons, press on. You are likely to identify many of the problems that make your life difficult and the organization's functioning expensive. Unfortunately, like many other business problems, recognizing commons problems does not solve them.

The major obstacle to overcoming commons problems is the issue of justice.

Participants in a commons view their rights to graze their sheep, take 15 percent of the budget, or occupy the tenth floor as God-given. This would not be a problem if *responsibilities* (to maintain the commons, earn the 15 percent, or subsidize the space) were associated with the claimed rights. This is not the case in a commons. When it comes time to reduce rights or to attach correlative responsibilities, each party feels that it is losing a right and gaining a responsibility for having done nothing that it considers wrong.

Any proposal to restrict access to a commons is viewed as *unjust* by at least some of those who expect unimpeded access. In the case of the common pasture, rationing access to the pasture on the basis of herd size will raise cries of injustice on the part of those who have small herds. On the other hand, if the pasture's usage is taxed, those with large herds will contend that they are unjustly penalized for success. Attempts to block access to information commons raise cries of "You are impeding free inquiry for commercial reasons!" and "We need that information to make loans, preserve national security, and calculate the mortality rates!"

What happens when the pasture reaches capacity and disaster is imminent? The herdsmen may call a meeting to determine a formula for limiting access to the pasture. They will not reach agreement. Any restriction of a herdsman's right to the commons will be viewed as unjust. This leaves two solutions.

One way out of a commons trap is for someone (typically a government) to introduce some factor to realign the interests of participants in the commons. This is intended to produce an outcome that someone (usually called "the common good") will be satisfied with. It will also produce an outcome that most participants in the commons will be dissatisfied with, since someone else is telling them what their best interests are. And there is no responsibility in this approach. It is a statement that we cannot manage ourselves, so you manage us. For example, when a river is polluted by factories along its banks, the government finally steps in and says, "OK, it's cleanup time." The factories responsible for the pollution have taken no responsibility for finding a solution and, because they are being "forced to clean up the river," view their cleanup efforts more as punishment than as a form of responsibility.

The other way out of a commons problem is responsibility. We must let responsibility back in if organizations are to function ethically and efficiently. But how do we bring forth responsibility without the government forcing it upon us?

I recommend a two-step approach to addressing commons problems and other hard problems of ethics and responsibility:

1. First, apply ethical tools to determine what you want to accomplish.
2. Then, create conditions in which that approach becomes practical.

The summary statement of this approach is: Use ethics to ask key questions, and then be purposeful. Let us review some of the ethical tools for implementing this approach.

Three ethical models

Tools are used for a purpose. The purpose of these tools is to allow managers to take ownership of the ethical issues that affect them and to build businesses that are better in the broadest sense, economically and ethically. The way to take ownership of ethical issues is to use ethical tools to ask questions that clarify where you and the organization stand and what you want to accomplish.

Three important ethical tools are end-point ethics, rule ethics, and social contract ethics. These models provide questions to guide managers in making decisions.

End-point ethics   In its most plausible form, end-point ethics says that a person or organization should do that which promotes the greatest balance of good over harm for everyone affected. The thinking manager uses end-point ethics to ask of a proposed action:

1.   What is in this course of action for me?
2.   What is in it for the others who are affected?

These questions focus attention on the stakeholders in a decision, including yourself.

The first step in an end-point decision process is to determine what stakeholder groups are critically affected by the decision and how they are affected.

Identifying stakeholder groups is a difficult process. The end-point approach demands that you press hard to identify stakeholder groups that do not immediately come to mind. Stakeholder groups always come to mind for themselves, and they demand their say. Identifying the stakeholders pays off. . . .

The second step of an end-point decision process is to identify alternative courses of action. Identify the alternatives you regard as most plausible. Then identify the alternatives that each stakeholder group regards as most plausible.

If practical, you should seek direct input from key stakeholder groups. This has two advantages. First, you may find that alternatives which you regard as optimal meet strong resistance in the stakeholder groups needed to implement them. Second, those with a different stake in the decision may see viable alternatives that you overlooked. It is as wise to listen to the consumers of decisions as it is to listen to the consumers of products.

Do not confuse end-point ethics with its offspring, cost-benefit analysis. There is a fine but critical distinction between the two. Because a cost-benefit analysis should result in a numerical assessment of whether the benefits of an action exceed the costs, the focus of cost-benefit analysis is narrowed to factors measurable in numerical terms. In contrast, the strength of end-point ethics is that it includes all factors that affect success.

End-point ethics is similar to cost-benefit analysis in that it takes quantifiable results into consideration, but end-point ethics goes farther. It takes the intangible but efficacious factors into account. . . . Tom Peters often says that in business, soft is hard. He means that factors which are hard to quantify often have the most effect on the bottom line. End-point ethics agree, adding that soft is sometimes hard with respect to the ethical bottom line as well.

The manager who uses end-point ethics is left with a lot of information and the need to make a decision. The manager knows who he is dealing with, the options available, and what's in the options for all concerned. In our terms, the ground rules of value have been brought to the surface. These determine what outcomes have what value for each stakeholder group. But the ground rules of evaluation, which define the *bounds of action* in pursuit of value, have not been heard from. That is the job of ethics.

Rule ethics   Rule ethics says that a person or organization should do what valid ethical principles require. Further, a person or organization should refrain from doing anything contrary to valid ethical principles. This does not tell you much unless you know what the valid ethical principles are. There are as many opinions about valid principles as there are ideologies, which is to say unmanageably many.

You can unravel this knot by building on the stakeholder process of end-point ethics. Once you have identified key stakeholder groups, correlate with each group its ethical code, or specific rule ethics. The thinking manager uses rule ethics to ask of proposed actions:

1. Which of my ground rules are potentially in conflict with this action?
2. Which of the ground rules of stakeholders are potentially in conflict with this proposed action?

This enables you to spot points of resistance to decisions not uncovered by specifying the interests of each group. If you are dealing with environmental groups, political bodies, or the media, knowing the ethical codes of these groups will help you anticipate their responses to your actions. These groups often act in ways that cannot be viewed as self-interested. You must unravel their ethical codes to anticipate their actions.

Groups that act from ideology rather than interest are seldom accurately anticipated by business. For example, developers often try to argue for a new project in terms of documentable benefits, only to be surprised by outraged citizens and governmental opposition. These groups can be anticipated in rule-ethical terms by taking a measure of their codes, or rules. . . . Some American firms succeed in the Orient; many do not. One significant success factor is the ability to read the ground rules of the stakeholder groups in these markets: Learn the ethical operating systems of those you deal with, and try speaking to them through compatible ethical software.

In discussing rule ethics, there is an important distinction between categorical rules and prima facie rules. Categorical rules allow absolutely no exceptions. Most ethical rules are not categorical.

For example, the rule that one should keep promises has clear exceptions. A manager who promises an employee a raise only to find out later than the firm is on the verge of bankruptcy is obligated to break his promise. The manager's obligation to act in the interests of the firm takes precedence. And other obligations, for example, defending the national interest, take precedence over the obligation

---

Who's who on the ethics front

For the past few years, a popular sport among business professors, management theorists and consultants has been coming up with lists of the "best" companies and their distinguishing attributes. Unsurprisingly, we were able to ferret out a couple of lists of companies characterized as highly ethical *and* successful organizations.

Although James O'Toole, author of *Vanguard Management: Redesigning the Corporate Future*, derides such list-making as an "executive parlor game," he, too, lists what he calls "Vanguard" corporations: Atlantic Richfield, Control Data, Dayton-Hudson, John Deere, Honeywell, Levi-Strauss, Motorola and Weyerhauser. . . .

What distinguishes the Vanguard, as O'Toole calls these leading companies, from the pack? A philosophy of management that embodies abstract concepts like "balance, integration, harmony, coherence and justice," according to O'Toole. He also offers a list of characteristics the Vanguard hold in common:

1. *They try to satisfy all of their stakeholders.* "The Vanguard believe that shareholders are best served in the long run when corporations attempt to satisfy the legitimate claims of *all* the parties that have a stake in their companies: consumers, employees, suppliers, dealers, special interest groups, host communities, governments, as well as shareholders."

2. *They are dedicated to high purpose.* "At the Vanguard there is commitment in word and deed to a higher purpose: These corporations exist to provide society with the goods and services it needs, to provide employment, and to create a surplus of wealth (profit) with which to improve the nation's general standard of living and quality of life. In this view, profit is the means, not the end, of corporate activity."

3. *They are committed to learning.* "The Vanguard corporations have discovered from the school of hard knocks that it is far better to practice preventive medicine. . . . to become a *learning organization*. And since there is no static body of corporate knowledge to master—no set of rules or principles that will lead all corporations to success—the Vanguard have discovered that they must *learn continually* from the changing environment. Their teachers are their many stakeholders."

4. *They try to be the best at everything they do.* "The Vanguard companies . . . [are] out to beat the world and won't let up until they are the best at *everything* they do. Each . . . has a chronic,

to act in the better interests of the firm. The distinction between prima facie and categorical rules would be of only intellectual interest were it not for the skill that critics of business display in exploiting it and for the lack of skill that business displays in responding to such critics.

A strategy for attacking business on ethical grounds is to indict

---

healthy dissatisfaction with the level of their varius achievements; they have institutionalized the process of change."

These philosophical orientations depend upon neither charismatic nor entrepreneurial management, O'Toole emphasizes. Rather, the Vanguard are led by managers who exhibit moral courage, e.g., the courage to change direction when all is going well; the courage to hire brilliant subordinates and allow them to shine; the courage to be an innovative subordinate; the courage to stick to their values in tough times; and the courage to resist pressure for short-term action.

In his book *The Hard Problems of Management: Gaining the Ethics Edge*, Mark Pastin also mentions several representatives from his international list of 25 "high-ethics, high-profit" organizations: Cadbury Schweppes, 3M, Atlantic Richfield, Motorola, Hilby Wilson, Inc., Northern Chemical Co., Interwestern Management and Apple Computer. He also boils down their attributes, philosophies, management practices or what have you, to four principles with a slightly different emphasis:

1. "High-ethics firms are at ease interacting with diverse internal and external stakeholder groups. The ground rules of these firms make the good of these stakeholder groups part of the firm's own good."
2. "High-ethics firms are obsessed with fairness. Their ground rules emphasize that the other person's interests count as much as their own."
3. "In high-ethics firms, responsibility is individual rather than collective, with individuals assuming personal responsibility for actions of the firm. These firms' ground rules mandate that individuals are responsible to themselves."
4. "The high-ethics firm sees its activities in terms of a purpose. This purpose is a way of operating that members of the firm value. And purpose ties the firm to its environment."

Both authors offer a caveat to their lists of admirable companies. Perhaps O'Toole says it best: "None of these companies fully adheres to the principles I describe. . . . I cite them as examples. . . . Lord knows I don't do so because they have achieved perfection."

business for violating a commonly recognized prima facie rule. The violation is vividly documented—but not the prima facie character of the rule or the extenuating circumstances....

Rule ethics advises that you reverse engineer your decisions, the decisions of others, and the decisions of organizations in order to determine your evaluation ground rules and those of others. But rule ethics leaves you in the same basic position as end-point ethics, with information and the need to decide and act. It adds a crucial element to the picture—the bounds defining acceptable actions for different groups—but it does not tell you how to move the boundaries to remove conflicts and, perhaps, to get a better deal. Social contract ethics addresses the nature of basic agreements and how they can be shifted.

Social contract ethics   A social contract is an implicit agreement about the basic principles or ethics of a group. Another way of looking at this is to say that, at the level groups, ground rules are a matter of implicit agreement. We find ourselves in a web of implicit agreements whenever we enter an organization. If these agreements are unbalanced, favoring some groups at the expense of others, the disfavored groups work to undermine the agreements. Social contract ethics provides a test for determining whether a contract is sound: *A contract is sound if parties to the contract would enter the contract freely and fairly.*

How can you tell whether the members of an organization would agree to the contracts of the organization freely and fairly? The thinking manager uses social contract ethics to ask:

1.   Do I agree to this contract or do I just live with it?
2.   If I were to occupy the position of a lower-level manager or employee, would I accept this contract?
3.   If I were a higher-level manager, would I accept this contract?

Look at it this way: If you were to have an equal chance of being assigned to a different rank in the organization, would you be satisfied with the contract as it applies to the ranks you might hold? Assume the positions of the various parties that live by the contract, and assess the contract from their perspectives.

What is the price of not recognizing the implicit agreements? If you do not know the agreements by which your organization operates, it is difficult to institute significant changes. Significant changes in organizations generally shift the social contract for those factions in the organization that are critical to implementing the change. If the shift is not perceived to be fair, these factions will resist the change. Their resistance is not always effective, but it is always expensive.

For example, problems occurred when Motorola attempted to change its culture without auditing its social contract. Motorola wanted to establish a culture of participation. Workers liked it and accepted it, for the culture change implied a shift in agreements that favored them; they got more pay, more respect, and more say in their working conditions. But the program stalled at middle management. The middle managers perceived that the line workers had gained advantages at their expense. Middle managers had to put in more time, listen to countless suggestions, and work harder for the same pay. Moreover, their outside options diminished. They resisted the change because of the agreement shift implicit in it. Middle managers are effective resistors.

The Motorola case underscores the close connection between the cultures of organizations and their social contracts (agreements). Social contracts are carried by the cultures of organizations and indeed constitute the operating core of the culture. That is why culture change, as now practiced, is difficult; it is attempted over the dead body of the ethical agreements at the core of the culture. On the other hand, organizations that manage ethical agreements can succeed while managing little else. The reason is simple: If the agreements are sound, the organization is willing to do its job without an undue measure of control, force, or atta-boying. . . .

If you ignore the agreements, you will find it extremely difficult to effect basic change in your organization. Everyone who does not know whether he or she will be treated fairly will have a stake in resisting the change. On the other hand, if you make a clear commitment to fair agreements, radical change is within your reach. If you know you are not going to lubricate the wheels of change, you can enjoy it. . . .

Think about the basic agreements (social contracts) in your organization. Establish and stand by agreements that are good for you and your firm. Be sure you would work under the agreements voluntarily. The changing nature of organizations is a fact; so is the changing nature of the basic technologies underlying business. Both facts make establishing fair agreements more difficult, and more important. Since organizations are rapidly becoming organizations by agreement, you might as well start managing the agreements.

Upholding agreements is not a basis for the activities of any business—it is a precondition for conducting these activities. And you can only establish a fair agreement if you are operating in a context in which people will be responsible to the agreement. Responsibility cannot be established by our ethical models. In fact, it cannot be established by any models.

The key ingredient

The key ingredient that moves us from models and analysis to decision and action is purpose. To find purpose, we must grasp the distinction between goals and purposes. Esoteric? Perhaps. But this distinction not only provides a place to stand in decision and action; it also unlocks the mystery of strategy.

A *goal* is a target towards which one aims. A goal no longer exists once it is hit, or missed. Goals answer the questions: Why are you doing that? Where do you except this company to be in one year? Five years? Goals are typically economic in form and include a target date. You must know whether or not you made the goal at some point; otherwise, you had no goal.

When one set of goals is exhausted, we must think of new goals. Where will they come from? Consultants? Management retreats? Organizations are often unclear where the next set of goals is coming from, and they often formulate unreachable or hopelessly vague goals. The problem is that goals must be set in terms of purpose if they are to fit the organization and gain the support of those charged with implementing the goals.

A *purpose* is a way of being or functioning viewed as valuable in itself. A purpose makes a value (as in a ground rule of value) specific and operational. If my purpose is to have computers support thinking rather than just data collection and manipulation, then this purpose makes concrete for me the value of being a thinker. . . .

Organizations also have purposes. The thinking manager seeking to know company purposes asks:

1. Why is the existence of this company worthwhile?
2. Why should I and others in the firm perform tasks and seek company goals with maximum commitment?

These questions are philosophical, but the need to address them is concrete. Purposes give a company a sense of who it is, where its goals come from, and why trying hard matters.

Remember that purpose answers one of our most important questions: When you have collected the information and done the analysis, where do you stand to decide and act? The answer is: Stand on your purpose. No one can tell you how to decide. But you can consult your purpose as a foundation—as an assurance that your decisions and actions collectively have meaning.

Once managers and employees accept the purpose of a company as worthwhile, they will assume individual responsibility. They will quit pointing fingers and begin blocking commons problems. They will think short-run or long-run, as appropriate to the problems they face. They will manage and work purposefully.

If asked, "How many organizations are purposeful?" I would cite Apple Computer, Bell Laboratories, 3M, Control Data Corporation, and Mrs. Field's Cookies. But the list is not long. Why? Even if the top management sees a purpose for the firm, it is not the firm's purpose until it moves down the line.

But purposes cannot be inculcated. Inculcating purpose makes no more sense than inculcating individuality. Top management must speak to the purposes and ground rules of the organization's members in order to produce an organization-individual alignment. This is the problem of responsibility in organizations. Each individual must be responsible for the purpose.

What is responsibility? How do you spread it? Is it an individual or collective matter?

Taking responsibility for getting responsibility

The single most important question the thinking manager can ask about any organization is: Who is responsible here?

Responsibility is the issue in almost every hard management problem, ethical or otherwise. This idea is not novel, just unpopular. Peter Drucker, in a retrospective on his work, puts responsibility front and center when he says: "I stressed all along that organization does not deal with power but with responsibility. This is the one keynote of my work that has remained constant over more than 40 years" (Peter Drucker, "Drucker on Drucker," *New Management* [Winter 1985]: 8). Drucker is right. But none of his ideas has received less attention or uptake. It is as if the word *responsibility* jams the mental circuits.

Responsibility is a complex concept that we all have a hard time understanding. One reason is that true responsibility, if understood, is very demanding. It is easy to talk about "taking responsibility" if you can use the phrase to fault others without getting the message yourself. Another reason is that responsibility challenges our entire way of looking at the world by forcing us to deal with paradoxes and to accept the idea that creativity is a part of plain old responsibility.

Responsibility requires *effectiveness, independence,* and *intention* (acting from purpose). You cannot be responsible if you are ineffective; if you cannot do it, you cannot be responsible for doing it. To be responsible, you must act independently of where the payoffs are. Payoffs are unlikely to track the requirements of responsible action in even the best situations. The only way to act independently is to act for a purpose that makes acting independently worth it to you.

Acting for a purpose that makes acting independently worth it to you is a compressed statement of exactly what ethical management is.

It is easy to pull the elements of responsibility together if you make one simple observation: People take responsibility for what they create. People will work hard—for less money, and above their abilities—if they are creating a new company (Apple), a new computer (Data General), or a new way of working together (Jaguar PLC). Creativity is literally doing something outside of the domain of the laws by which the world predictably works; the ancients said creativity is bringing something into being from nothing. That, of course, is impossible according to our scientific world view but still quite necessary.

The very ideas of responsibility and creativity force paradox on us. Paradox is good for the manager because it forces thinking outside of the parameters that lock in competitors. If you ask good questions—if you are a thinking manager—you find a lot of paradoxes. Learn to love them, or you will have to quit asking. One paradox is that of individual versus group responsibility. This paradox excuses more irresponsible conduct than does alcoholism. We resolve this paradox by embracing it.

The individual is the source of responsibility since the individual is the source of creativity. But the creative individual cannot create by himself, so he or she creates the group as co-creators. For example: Some members of the department in which I work teach poorly; I am an excellent teacher; I am not responsible for teaching that I do not do. Why do some colleagues teach poorly? Perhaps it is due to motivation, lack of basic skills, a reward system that undervalues teaching, internal politics, marital problems, and so on. *How can I be responsible for these things?* If asked sincerely, this is a powerful question. I can be responsible by participating in the hiring and promotion of teachers lacking basic skills. I can be responsible for lack of attention to what my colleagues do, for acquiescence in a reward system that undervalues teaching, and for a lack of sensitivity to politics and personal problems. I am not so much responsible for the existence of problems as I am for the existence of unsolved problems. If doing good teaching is a purpose for me, and if I am effective in pursuing this purpose, *I am responsible for creating solutions to these problems.*

Any manager who sincerely and aggressively asks, "How can I be responsible for these things?" will find very many good answers.

Ethical Issues for the Public Manager

James S. Bowman

This discussion ... is generally exploratory in nature, providing basic tools, background information, and critical standards to approach and evaluate ethical questions in the civil service. It is not intended to serve as a treatise on ethics or philosophy, inasmuch as work is available in those fields to permit further analysis of the concepts mentioned here. In the face of the tendency to avoid direct confrontation with moral problems, to debate ethical issues without conclusion, and to dwell excessively on pious platitudes, the focus is, instead, on the application of ethical principles to organizations. Since ethics asks questions about broad public purpose to guide conduct toward human welfare, analysis of these problems mandates action.

The first section examines the definition and evolution of the study of ethics in government. This is followed by an investigation of individual professional values in organizational settings.... The chapter concludes with a commentary on the future of ethics. Any such overview does not "solve" moral problems. That, of course, is not in the cards, given the inscrutability of these questions. However, in the light of humankind's ancient curiosity about ethics and contemporary ethical issues, the study is a timely analysis of the administrative implications of this subject. The problem addressed here is starkly simple: the legitimacy of the state and its ability to govern.

Definition and evolution of the field

The events of the 1970s served as a catalyst for questioning values,

Reprinted from William B. Eddy, ed., *A Handbook of Organization Management.* Copyright © 1981 by Marcel Dekker, Inc., New York. Permission courtesy of Marcel Dekker, Inc.

priorities, and institutions in American life. "Ethics" is very clearly a term of great rhetorical power in the nation's politics. Although it may be true that for years it was a sentimental topic of conversation, today sound professional ethics is a practical necessity for administrative effectiveness.

When faced with moral predicaments in daily management, however, inchoate responses frequently result. As Stephen K. Bailey (1960:4) has pointed out:

> Although almost every issue with which [the administrator] must deal is charged with ethical dilemmas, it is rare that the executive has either the time, the context, or the liver for constructing balanced ethical judgments. He does what he must. . . . [He] tends . . . to "fly by the seat of his pants." . . . If we are talking about the real world, then we are talking . . . about the *inarticulate* moral premises of the office holder. . . . (see also Mintzberg, 1975).

Most officials have never been prepared to employ patterns of ethical reasoning, and simpy are not conversant in philosophy or ethics. In order to seek a better understanding of the problem confronting the manager, it is important to have a historical and analytical background to it, because this helps move the author and the reader beyond a personal, intuitive, and moralistic perspective on public administration.

Before defining the topic of inquiry—ethics—several general propositions or observations that underlie its study seem appropriate. First, concern for proper behavior in government can be traced back to the dawn of civilization (Caiden and Caiden, 1979:477). Disreputable conduct has been condemned in every generation and by all societies; indeed, suspicion of authority may well be the natural order of things. In this country, the animus began with the American Revolution and has continued ever since.

Second, it is essential to recognize that the concern for ethics is pervasive. If democracy is rule by the people, and government is getting things done through people, ethics penetrates all phases of public life. It follows, finally, that the question of civic virtue in contemporary government cannot be left to the exhortations of moralists and crusaders. Although appeals to conscience, inspirational essays, and accusatory polemics may have some value, they do little to describe and explain behavior in the public service. If the study of "ethical issues for the public manager" is to be fruitful, it must concentrate on problems central to management. Civil servants themselves must therefore contribute to development standards for professional administration.

Definition of management ethics   The study of ethics may be an established discipline, but its application and integration into contemporary government is just beginning. Although one of the exceptional characteristics of human beings is their moral behavior, there has been a general reluctance on the part of students of organizations to give appropriate consideration to this fact. There are, for instance, few analytical models of the subject to help guide one through the maze of reality, to develop generalizations, and draw conclusions. In both practice and theory, the ethical implications of administrative and political conduct remain largely unexplored. As Dwight Waldo and Patrick Hennigan (1979:86) point out, the professional literature "almost totally ignores ethical conduct in organizational management" (see also Donaldson and Waller, 1980).[1] It is little wonder, then, that although many public service ethics programs were established at a time of great moral concern (i.e., Vietnam and Watergate), a majority of concerned scholars reported that they "were in a quandary about how to proceed" (Steinfels, 1977:3).

Yet no one is entirely free of moral codes, certainly not managers who are more affluent and better educated than the general public. Available evidence clearly demonstrates that they are interested in ethics and can identify them as being associated with rules and standards, morals, right and wrong, and values of honesty and integrity (see, e.g., Newstrom and Ruch, 1975; Brenner and Molander, 1977; Hill, 1979).

Although almost every individual has little difficulty understanding the idea of ethics, it is not easy to define. Among the numerous attempts to explain its meaning, perhaps the best definition for the administrator is that ethics are a set of standards by which human actions are determined to be right or wrong. Stated differently, ethics may be seen as the rules governing moral conduct of the members of the organization or management profession.[2]

This inquiry into administrative ethics is guided by the following assumptions:

1. The practice of management generates ethical predicaments.
2. People are capable of choosing one course of action rather than another in dealing with these dilemmas.
3. Admirable behavior can be nurtured and directed in organizational settings.

"In essence," write Charles W. Powers and David Vogel (1980:1), "ethics is concerned with clarifying what constitutes general welfare and the kind of conduct necessary to promote it."

Evolution of the field   What, then, of the evolution of the study of government ethics? Although the methodological problems noted above have retarded growth in the field, perhaps more significant is the manner in which the subject has been approached historically.[3] Beginning with one of the first American political scientists and the father of the study of public administration, Woodrow Wilson (1887), it was recognized that the quintessential problem of U.S. government was the reconciliation of democracy with administration, the relationship between politics and execution of policy.

Although early political scientists, like the founders of other social sciences, often aspired to a new science of morality, in doing so they joined good government advocates who insisted that administration could be divorced from politics. If public administration could be nonpartisan, it was reasoned, it could then be subjected to scientific analysis. The politics/administration concept devolved into a rigid intellectual dichotomy, and as a theory of administration in democracy, replaced the spoils system as political orthodoxy. Congruent with the tenets of Weberian bureaucratic hierarchy, the dualism obscured ethical dimensions of public administration since it placed most administrators beyond the province of moral responsibility.

In a time of great concern over professional status and confidence in the scientific method, the abdication of social responsibility that accompanies the abandonment of values was one of the consequences of the period. Political science, the parent discipline of public administration, made the fateful shift toward the science and disciplinary model as against the professional. An empirical approach to politics would make it as scientific as the other social sciences and perhaps even the natural sciences. Value-free behavioral inquiry promised to discover verifiable laws of politics while eschewing any overt reformist convictions. Scholars interested in the organization of government drew inspiration from business management and ultimately developed scientific formulae for administration. Laws of political behavior and principles of administration would join the modern science of government.

Undergirded by the dichotomy, the study of government evolved with little attention to purpose or values. "A concern for ethics," wrote Donald P. Warnick (1980:38), "signified either a return to the spongy speculations of yesteryear or a mass of conjectures that are unverified, arcane, and thus intellectually suspect." "Values appeared," according to William Lee Miller (1977:13), "only if they were somebody else's and could be counted." The era increasingly looked like the "iron cage" prophesied by Weber, as little attention was paid to the growing Leviathan that supplied grants to the profession.

The demise of the politics/administration dichotomy in the 1940s, the suspicion of value-free science in the 1960s, and contemporary ethical problems have converged to make it evident that theoreticians and practitioners form decisions on the basis of both science and morality. Nicholas Henry (1978:133) stated that by the late 1970s these developments made students of public administration "cognizant of the disquieting notion that a sense of ethics was a genuine need" in the field.

Thus, over the past century, ethics has moved from macromorality, intrinsic to the discipline, to near invisibility as a topic. It has only recently acquired a visible, if small and often uncertain presence, in public administration. The separation between ethics and administration had been scientifically as well as politically troublesome. The American dream, of which public administration had been so much a part, turned into a nightmare.

Although it may now be fashionable, relatively speaking, to study ethics, it will not be an easy task. Yet, if value differences are to be resolved by the democratic process, the ability to articulate what is at stake is required; the fact that judgments in this area are difficult to make should and does not stop them from being made.

The crisis of identity in the study and practice of the field stems from the fact that public administration "has no well-defined ideals" (Redford, 1958:ix). Public administration must be credible and comprehensive to both theoreticians and practitioners. Such authenticity implies that the administrative responses be a function of values. They are not merely inevitable, but constitute the irreducible nucleus of public administration (Hodgkinson, 1978). To the extent that ideas such as public trust are eroded, public administration loses what Waldo (1980:78) calls "its rich ethical aura." The administrator who allows his or her moral sense to atrophy, or who retreats to managerialism, relinquishes responsibility for nurturing professional ethics in organizational settings.

Professional ethics in an organizational setting

Democratic governance relies heavily on personal integrity and trust and confidence between the public and its officials. The citizenry, in fact, has been able to depend on the professional self-discipline of the majority of civil servants. William B. Eddy (1980:13) is surely correct when he argues that "credibility is an issue of individual responsibility, competence, congruence, and realistic goals—not of public relations campaigns and image building." Since each employee has the opportunity every day to take steps toward ethical behavior, many Americans believe that improper conduct can be explained principally in terms of individual morality and personal deficiencies.

However, to the extent that organizations put people in situations where they have discretion, even the most honest administrator may find it difficult to determine what is appropriate conduct. Very real dilemmas arise for the public servant when a collective consensus is lacking. Since the definition of right and wrong is highly diverse in pluralistic societies, and large differences in personal values of executives exist (e.g., England, 1975), it is not reasonable to assume that everyone knows what a moral judgment is. As case studies and surveys (e.g., Harris, 1978; Boling, 1978a:361) suggest, many managers are unable to handle the resulting ambiguities in a suitable manner. It is for these reasons that an exclusive emphasis on individual ethics is an inadequate foundation for understanding of managerial ethics, and for the identification and resolution of relevant administrative problems (for excellent statements of this position, see Boling, 1978b; Waters, 1978; Allen, 1980).

The public's unhappiness about ethical transgressions joined with confusion as to what constitutes unethical behavior demonstrates the need to clarify standards. Although many people have a sense of right and wrong, only when a large number of individuals come together can common expectations be established and achieved. That is, while behavior is a function of personal values, organizations, through their actions, endorse certain types of action. Individual conduct takes place in a social context. Employees may make decisions based on personal standards, but institutions define and control the situations in which these decisions are made. People's value systems, as a consequence, adapt to the environment in which they find themselves (England, 1975).

The difficulty is that most administrators believe that organizations do not foster ethical behavior. Robert F. Allen (1980:30) reports:

Of the 1,500 respondents to our surveys, taken in a wide variety of organizations, ... less than 10 percent felt that the organizations in our society tend to encourage their members to behave ethically, honestly, and humanely. In fact, more than 65 percent agreed with the opposite statement—that [they] "tend to encourage their members to behave unethically, dishonestly, and inhumanely...."

Managers perceive that the bureaucratic environment is less ethical than their own values and beliefs, that they are under pressure to compromise personal standards to achieve organizational goals, and that their supervisors are interested only in results, not how they were obtained (see, e.g., Carroll, 1975; Bowman, 1976; Brenner and Molander, 1977).

One might expect that those with high moral character would be unable to operate effectively in an environment that provides few ethical guidelines to action. Strong systematic arrangements are not in place in government to provide a regularized means to address untoward actions that do arise (Kieffer, 1980). Although institutions frequently resent being embarrassed by wrongdoing, they seldom act to discourage future improprieties. When interactions among people and institutions no longer provide normal opportunities for the exercise of integrity, agencies must assume at least partial responsibility for the ethical conduct of their employees. It is not sufficient for an individual to be convinced of his or her own rectitude and integrity. Instead, some kind of institutional basis for professional conduct is necessary. A fundamental change in the passive philosophy underlying ethical standards in government must be fostered (Comptroller General of the United States, 1978).

Recognizing that human beings are not faultless, it is critical to try to live up to the best kinds of standards that can be realistically established. Although an effective system will not produce perfect people, an inadequate system will produce criminals. The test for the administrator, then, is to understand just what she or he confronts, and devise ways to make that reality manageable. Managers, as moral custodians of collective goals, are strategically placed to recognize factors that promote and inhibit ethical behavior. Accordingly, they should be held responsible for providing a foundation for responsible behavior....

There is a compelling need for clearer guidance in identifying major sources of unethical conduct and for a clarification of significant problems to make public employees more sensitive to actual and potential problems that challenge government as a whole. Agencies should undertake a variety of steps to alert their officials to ethical dilemmas, among them:

1.   Initiation of an imaginative training program
2.   Development of an enforceable code of conduct
3.   Establishment of channels and encouragement of professional dissent

Careful thought in advance about ethical problems will lead to a working consensus on what is acceptable conduct, and thereby avoid inappropriate behavior arising from ignorance. The administrative task is to prevent the necessity for whistle-blowing, enforce ethical codes, and provide training opportunities. When organizations employ professionals, in other words, they have the obligation to provide support structures for professional actions.

If an agency desires ethical conduct, the first thing it should do is to have a meeting of top management. The head of the department should explain that she or he does not want anyone in the organization to engage in unethical practices, and that training programs, codes of ethics, and professional dissent will be developed and supported. It should be affirmed that serving the public interest is a vocation requiring intellectual excellence and moral integrity. If top managers do not understand this, resignations should be requested (Hill, 1976:13). Such an initiative, albeit drastic, will bring about fundamental—not cosmetic—changes in the way business is done in the agency. Exemplary behavior on the part of senior managers plus the threefold program of action noted above will keep moral discourse alive.

Examples of the failure of reform efforts are not hard to find, and cynics delight in recounting them. These efforts fail when they are but window dressing from the outset meant to please or exhaust employees, or when they are turned into manipulative management tools (Bok, 1980:292; Feldman, 1980:477). A great deal of energy is expended in bewailing the impossibility of combatting waste, corruption, and mismanagement in government. Such energy would be put to better use in employing techniques to address the problem. Ethics in government is a matter of social relations; substantial improvement can be expected only if organizations and their members act. The release or promotion of those whose conduct warrants it is a matter of vigorous personnel management.

Organizations must, in their own interest, come to grips with the complexity of their operations that seems to make it possible for questionable practices to flourish. The problem of administrative ethics is one of discretion in the pursuit of the public good. Agencies must plant and nourish a standard of ethical performance that takes into account the realities of everyday management. Ignoring the problem will not make it go away, and may well make it worse. Surely it is better for administrators to be aware of the complexities of important issues than to act on unexamined premises. The oath of office creates a moral community among government employees that demands an ethical commitment to the public trust. The challenge is to instill in the civil service a program of action that builds upon that oath.

Future of ethics in government

If corruption, as a permanent companion of power, is a part of the human condition, ethics in government is and will remain a subject of controversy. In this era of massively complex government, official deviance will become an increasingly vexatious social problem.[4] Whether or not this will lead to significant changes in political institutions remains to be seen; applied managerial ethics can be used to seek reform as well as to provide rationalizations for dubious activities. "Ethics" may sound purely moralistic, but fundamentally it just means the kind of behavior that enables people in a free society to live together.

Although some observers claim that there is less corruption today than in the past, corrupt practices were usually subject to the existing standards in which they occurred. There is clearly today a deeper trouble in society, as there has been disintegration of social consensus. Few collective standards exist in which confidence can be invested. Understanding how events relate to each other is no longer an easy matter for concerned people. Contemporary concern with the scope of government should focus not only on what it can do to citizens, but also the public's ability to make it work for people.

The problem is that this ability is gradually being lost, since there has been a steady erosion of responsibility in American politics (The End of Consensus, 1980).

In the context, it must be acknowledged that this study is hardly novel and its analysis of ethical problems unexceptional. And that is exactly the point. As Gerald Caiden (1980:23) has argued, the remedies are known. The problem is not so much ignorance of what needs to be done, but doing it. The resources that government has to bring to bear and the role it can play in addressing the issue are substantial. The problem is the lack of will or incentive to elevate public service ethics and implement them.

Accordingly, much remains to be done to achieve the integration of ethics and management. However, since the study of administrative ethics is still in its pioneer stage, the agenda ahead is full of exciting possibilities; until it matures, practice is likely to remain uneven and incomplete (Caiden, 1978:117). The need should strengthen as governments continue to experience the pathologies of large-scale bureaucracies. The managerial challenge is to reconcile, not merely accept, the conflicts between individual integrity and administrative demands. Ethics, like management, is an art. Although there may be no authoritative interpretation of management ethics—the uncertainty that pervades management includes moral issues—it is important that administrators accept the obligation to put themselves in touch with the concerns of the American people.

"All ethical questions ultimately revert to propositions about the nature of man. The underlying complexity of ethical questions stems from the fact that man is morally ambiguous and teleologically inscrutable" (Bailey, 1960:10). A nation's political health is connected directly with its sense of the future. If Walter Lippman (1970:296) was right in arguing that "the American ideal of government as public trust represents a long step ahead in the evolution of man, then it must be believed that man is capable of continuing the journey to responsible democracy." It seems evident that government cannot expect the support of the public unless it adopts the attitudes and actions discussed here in the near future.

Notes

1. There appear to be significant methodological reasons for this neglect (Caiden and Caiden, 1979:479–480). Information is hard to obtain, partly because it is not always in the self-interest of leaders to expose ethical problems. Accordingly, there are few reliable indicators of the scope and magnitude of these issues. Notorious scandals, for instance, get more exposure than ubiquitous, persistent forms of corruption that seldom come to light. There are disagreements about identification, measurement, causes, importance, value, and remedies in

administrative ethics research. The state of the art, in a word, is primitive.

2. Since the intent here is to call attention to the practical significance of the term, these definitions, which are based on Webster, seem satisfactory. Scholastic objections acknowledged, the words "values," "morals, " and "ethics" can be used in the text as synonyms. For a brief conceptual distinction, which is then disregarded, see Waldo (1980:99fn).

3. Small portions of this analysis are excerpted and revised from Bowman (1980a).

4. There is no proof that unethical conduct is growing, but given the magnitude of government and the proliferation of indictments, it is evident that the opportunities and incentives for corruption are substantial.

References

Allen, R.F. (1980). The IK in the Office. *Organizational Dynamics 8*:27–41.

Bailey, S.K. (1960). Ethics and the Politician. Occasional paper, Center for the Study of Democratic Institutions, Santa Barbara, Calif.

Bok, S. (1980). Whistleblowing and Professional Responsibilities. In *Teaching Ethics in Higher Education*, D. Callahan and S. Bok (eds.). New York: Plenum, pp. 277–295.

Boling, T.E. (1978a). The Management Ethics "Crisis": An Organizational Perspective. *Academy of Management Review 3*:360–365.

Boling, T.E. (1978b). Organizational Ethics: Rules, Creativity, and Idealism. In *Management Handbook for Public Administration*, J. W. Sutherland (ed.). New York: Van Nostrand Reinhold, pp. 221–253.

Bowman, J.S. (1976). Managerial Ethics in Business and Government. *Business Horizons 19*:48–54.

Brenner, S.N., and Molander, E.A. (1977). Is the Ethics of Business Changing? *Harvard Business Review 58*:57–71.

Caiden, G. (1978). Administrative Reform: A Prospectus. *International Review of Administrative Science 44*:106–120.

Caiden, G. (1980). Public Maladministration and Bureaucratic Corruption: A Comparative Perspective. Paper presented at the National Conference on Fraud, Waste, and Abuse, Pittsburgh, Pa.

Caiden, G., and Caiden, N. (1979). Coping with Administrative Corruption: An Academic Perspective. In *Dynamics of Development—An International Perspective*, S.K. Shama (ed.). New Delhi: Concept Publishing, pp. 478–494.

Carroll, A.B. (1975). Managerial Ethics: A Post-Watergate View. *Business Horizons 18*:75–80.

Comptroller General of the United States (1978). *Federal Agencies Can, and Should Do More to Combat Fraud in Government Programs*. Washington, D.C.: General Accounting Office.

Donaldson, J., and Waller, M. (1980). Ethics and Organization. *Journal of Management Studies 17*:34–55.

Eddy, W.B. (1980). Credibility of the Public Manager: A Personal/Professional Issue. *Bureaucrat 9*:11–14.

The End of Consensus (1980). *Daedalus 109*: entire issue.

England, G.W. (1975). *The Manager and His Values: An International Perspective from the United States, Japan, Korea, India, and Australia*. Cambridge, Mass.: Ballinger.

Feldman, D.L. (1980). Combatting Waste in Government. *Policy Analysis 6*:467–477.

Harris, C.E. (1978). Structuring a Workable Business Code of Ethics. *University of Florida Law Review XXX*:310–382.

Henry, N. (1978). *Public Administration and Public Affairs*, 2nd ed. Englewood Cliffs, N.J.: Prentice-Hall.

Hill, I. (1976). The Ethical Basis of Economic Freedom. Paper presented at National Leadership Conference of the American Medical Association, Chicago.

Hill, I. (1979). Interview. Ethics Resource Center, Washington, D.C.

Hodgkinson, C. (1978). *Towards a Philosophy of Administration*. New York: St. Martin's.

Kieffer, J.A. (1980). The Case for an Inspector General of the United States. *Bureaucrat 9*:11-22.

Lippman, W. (1970). A Theory About Corruption. In *Political Corruption: Readings in Comparative Analysis*, A.J. Heidenheimer (ed.). New York: Holt, Rinehart, and Winston, pp. 294-297.

Miller, W.L. (1977). Politics and Ethics. *Hastings Center Report 7*:13-14.

Mintzberg, H. (1975). The Manager's Job: Folklore and Fact. *Harvard Business Review 53*:49-61.

Newstrom, J.W., and Ruch, W.A. (1975). The Ethics of Management and the Management of Ethics. *Business Topics 23*:29-37.

Powers, C.W., and Vogel, D. (1980). *Ethics in the Education of Business Managers*. Hastings-on-Hudson, N.Y.: Hastings Center.

Redford, E. (1958). *Ideal and Practice in Public Administration*. University, Ala.: University of Alabama.

Steinfels, P. (1977). *The Place of Ethics in Schools of Public Policy*. New York: Hastings Center Report to the Ford Foundation.

Waldo, D. (1980). *The Enterprise of Public Administration: A Summary View*. Novato, Calif.: Chandler and Sharp.

Waldo, D., and Hennigan, P. (1979). Ethical Obligations of the Public Administrator: A Poorly Mapped Terrain. In *Ethics in the Public Service*, National Academy of Public Administration (ed.). Washington, D.C.: The Academy.

Warnick, D.P. (1980). *The Teaching of Ethics in the Social Sciences*. Hastings-on-Hudson, N.Y.: Hastings Center.

Waters, J.S. (1978). Catch 20.5: Corporate Morality as an Organizational Phenomenon. *Organizational Dynamics 6*:3-19.

Wilson, W.W. (1887). The Study of Administration. *Political Science Quarterly 2*:197-222.

Ethics Training

Clark Moeller

Ethics training is being provided in corporate training facilities. Allied Corporation has been offering a program of ethics training for the last several years in its Morristown, New Jersey, facilities. Cummings Engineering Corporation has employed professional ethicists to help its managers evaluate the ethical aspects of their day-to-day management problems. IBM and Lockheed Corporation are conducting ethics training. "Corporate ethics," claims A. W. Clausen, past president of BankAmerica, "has been historically and is now a moving, changing, and growing dimension of the total ethical values of the United States."[1]

Subordinate managers and employees are keenly interested in figuring out their boss's philosophy so they can adapt to his or her approach. The more clearly a manager can explain his or her management philosophy to the troops, the easier leadership becomes. Ethics training is one way of helping managers define their philosophy and find the common denominators that offer a meaningful and consistent approach to the problems that cascade upon them each day.

In this article, I will discuss the purpose and justification for ethics training as well as offer suggestions regarding its content and the conditions necessary for introducing ethics training in a corporate program.

First, however, it is worth noting that the emergence of ethics as a corporate and public concern is not a passing fad. It is a response to fundamental changes in our society. The technical revolution has created ethical dilemmas where none existed before. For example, genetic screening to identify blacks who are carriers of the sickle-cell anemia trait has been done by DuPont Company in order to identify employees who may be harmed by exposure to certain chemicals. This effort to promote employee safety has been challenged as just another way of institutionalizing job discrimination based on race. The laws have changed. The demands for equal employment opportunity, equal pay for equal work, and freedom from sexual harassment on the job are now being treated seriously. The laws have changed because important relationships in the workplace have changed—like the composition of the labor force. It's younger, more educated, more female, and reflects a changed ethnic mix. Furthermore, the majority of couples now bring in two paychecks, and jobs are more secure. Therefore, the balance of power between the employer and the employee has become more equal.

M. R. Cooper and colleagues summarize their findings on the changes in employee values by characterizing these changes as "ubiquitous, pervasive, and nontransient; any reversal is unlikely in the foreseeable future." These changes are like shifting sands underlying executive control. "The goal for management," Cooper et al. continue, "is to be aware of, and prepare for new and surfacing employee needs, before it is forced to take reactive, ignorant, and resistive postures."[2]

The companies that fail to adapt will be spending more time in courts on equal opportunity challenges and unemployment insurance claims. The company with a well-managed atmosphere will have a significant advantage in attracting and holding workers and managers in the future.

Purpose of ethics training

Until recently, ethics training was only found in colleges and universities. There are fundamental differences between the purposes of a university and those of a corporation. An appreciation of these differences will help promote mutuality of expectations between a university ethics teacher and a corporate management trainer who team-teach a course in management ethics.

A primary purpose of a university is to produce students capable of independent thought. A corporation should make a profit by producing a product or service. Although these differences seldom change how management training is presented in the university class or in the corporate training facility, this may be less true for ethics training.

The objectives for teaching an ethics course in a college, according to the Hastings Center, are "to provide students with those concepts and analytical skills that will enable them to grapple with

Table 1. First 51 ethics variables ranked in order of most frequent mention by total sample.

Rank	Variables ranked in order of most frequent mention	Percentage responding
1	Extortion, gifts, and kickbacks (employee's relationship to firm)	67.1
2	Conflict of interest	64.6
3	Illegal political payments	58.9
4	Obeying laws in general	56.8
5	Insider information	43.2
6	Illegal gifts and services	41.1
7	Bribery (firm's relationship to government)	36.8
8	Bribery (employee's relationship to firm)	34.3
9	Reporting full disclosure	33.6
10	Falsification of corporate accounts	27.9
11	"Other" (employee's relationship to firm)	26.4
12	Obeying antitrust laws	25.0
13	Moonlighting	24.6
14	Legal payments abroad	22.5
15	Secrecy	21.8
16	Knowledge of laws	21.8
17	"Other" (miscellaneous concerns)	21.8
18	Business in "different from us" nations	21.4
19	Kickbacks (firm's relationship to suppliers)	17.9
20	"Other" (firm's relationship to government)	16.1
21	Work safety	15.7
22	Equal employment opportunity	15.4
23	Commitment to local community	15.4
24	Fair pricing practices	15.1

broad ethical theory in attempting to resolve both personal and professional dilemmas, as well as to reflect on the moral issues facing the larger society.[3] In contrast, corporate efforts to guide behavior have been through corporate codes of ethics and indoctrination. "And rightly so," most CEOs would claim. "We're leading a team here, and we want the team members all going in the same direction!" However, the examples set by the behavior of top managers— what they say and the kinds of questions they ask—are the greatest influences. The structure of the organization and its management systems are the second significant influences. These set the stage or context for interpersonal behavior. A third influence, albeit a distant third, is the corporation's code of ethics. My own analysis of many corporate codes indicates that some are well written, but many are adopted as defensive policies aimed at protecting the corporate image rather than promoting ethical conduct by employees. Not surprisingly, there is a good deal of skepticism concerning the effectiveness of corporate codes of ethics.

Cutting across all of these—leadership by example, organization, and policies—is the influence of corporate training. Every soci-

Table 1. Continued.

Rank	Variables ranked in order of most frequent mention	Percentage responding
25	Fair wages	14.3
26	Management's obligation	14.3
27	Conflict of interest (firm's relationship to suppliers)	13.2
28	Unrecorded funds prohibited	13.2
29	Profits	12.9
30	To cooperate with government	12.5
31	"Other" (firm's relationship to customers)	12.1
32	Accurate advertising	11.8
33	Firm's social role	11.8
34	Morality in general	11.4
35	Management integrity	11.4
36	Working conditions	11.4
37	Job qualifications	11.1
38	"Other" (firm's relationship to employees)	11.1
39	Fraud, deception, etc.	11.1
40	Conspiracy	11.1
41	Job enrichment	10.7
42	Reciprocity	10.7
43	Affirmative action	10.7
44	Means to goals	10.7
45	Expenses	10.4
46	Unfair competition	10.4
47	Unethical competition	10.4
48	Quality products and services	10.4
49	Payola	9.6
50	Fair bidding	8.9
51	Free market commitment	8.9

Source: *An Analysis of Corporate Statements on Ethics and Behavior*, pp. 47, 49; prepared for The Standards of Performance Task Force, California Roundtable, June 1978, Robert Chatov and Associates, Snyder, N.Y. 14226.

ety and organization at least implicitly acknowledges that the educator is one of the principal guardians of its culture. However, in contrast to the university professor wrapped in the protective mantle of academic freedom, the corporate trainer faces fairly immediate feedback about the appropriateness and effectiveness of his or her training efforts. The performance standard of the bottom line is never very distant. In short, ethics training in a corporate environment must meet performance standards that are at least politically more demanding, if not necessarily academically more exacting, than those in a university.

Teaching college students to analyze ethical issues fits squarely within the oldest tradition of our universities. Teaching management ethics in corporations, on the other hand, is a relatively novel idea and needs a different justification. Ethics training within the corporation can promote control by top management, increase productivity, and improve the chances that managers and employees will obey corporate policies and the laws of the land. Furthermore, these objectives can be met by a fair and open analysis of ethical issues.

In order to argue this position and establish a framework for outlining the content of ethics training, I will begin by discussing how the ethical values of a corporation create its atmosphere and how the atmosphere influences employee productivity and management control.

Norms

Every group develops norms of behavior that increase each member's capacity to predict what the other members will do. This make communications more efficient and facilitates cooperation. Norms are a collective agreement about what is necessary to survive, what works, or how little needs to be done to get by. Corporations have norms that support their culture and others that create their atmosphere.

Since the terms *corporate atmosphere* and *corporate culture* are so frequently used interchangeably, some definitions will help dispel the fog. By corporate culture, I mean the behavior that develops as a result of offering a particular product or service. Banks, departments of social work, tool manufacturers, and advertising agencies are all culturally different. In contrast, the atmosphere of a corporation influences the quality of interpersonal relationships within the corporation and the effectiveness of executive control in directing subordinate staff. The atmosphere of a corporation is the summation of norms that are strongly influenced by top management behavior. Although the culture of a corporation does influence the routine of interpersonal relationships, it does so primarily through the patterns of communication that result from the technology and management systems used to produce the product or service. The atmosphere influences the quality of interpersonal relationships because it is created by the norms that define how people are valued.

Banks share a common cultural orientation to the marketplace. They have a similar technical vocabulary and recruit people with financial and accounting skills. In contrast, advertising people not only offer different services; they belong to different trade associations and even dress differently. Deal and Kennedy have described four different corporate cultural types: the macho cultures of venture capital, advertising, and television; the work hard/play hard cultures of real estate, automotive distribution, and door-to-door sales; the "bet-your-company" cultures of oil exploration, aircraft manufacturing, and computer design; and the process cultures of insurance, banking, and utilities.[4]

The lower one goes in an organization and the closer one gets to the first-line supervisor, the more atmosphere supersedes culture as a factor in executive control. The further employees are removed from participating in setting goals that shape a corporation's culture, the more they focus on the remaining opportunities available to improve their status. These often involve concerns about their rights, obligations, and justice.

Rights, obligations, and justice are, of course, ethical concepts. The fairness of a performance evaluation system, the confidentiality of proprietary information or personnel records, and the freedom to criticize are common issues. Announcing profit goals, setting monthly production targets, or defining improvements to be made during the year are essential to intelligent and humane management. However, like any powerful idea, managing for results becomes a weakness if it becomes a drag chain submerging other values. It is one thing for people to feel they are part of a team and, in that sense, a means to an end. It is another thing if people are valued only for their contribution to the end and, worse, when only the results are valued. Morale is the single most important influence on the employee's productivity. The single most important influence on the employee's morale is the relationship with his or her supervisor. And the single most important influence on the employee/supervisor relationship is the atmosphere of the organization. That atmosphere is sustained by the informal communications systems.

It's through informal chatting and joking that our work and social relationships are knitted together and that most recognition and prestige are awarded. It is also how acceptable behaviors are reinforced and unacceptable activity is punished. Even a small dose of mocking humor can usually elicit a slight cringe of humiliation or anger—sufficient for us to reassess our behavior. No one wants to be taken for a fool. Sociologist William Goode points out, "Expressing dispraise requires, at a minimum, several additional phases of action (counterargument, analysis, reconciliation, and so forth) before both parties can be turned to the previous flow of interaction.[5] Thus are boundaries of acceptable behavior defined, conformity to the group norms reinforced, and the language of membership taught. It's the content of gossip, the informal communications system, that reflects the values and norms of the organization.

The beauty of informal employee communications is that, through it, prestige and sanctions are awarded every so subtly, at the most strategic time, by almost any member of the group. There are no performance evaluation forms to be completed or records to file and only the slightest accountability. It's a neat system. However, although it is a self-correcting system, it is seldom a self-directing system. This is why the philosophy and commitment of top management are so important. A major component of any organization's values is how rights, obligations, and justice are determined.

The pervasive influence on this is top management's philosophy of management. This is why ethics training is central to management development. Being able to define and direct the norms that influence how people get along is a key to successful leadership.

Essential conditions for offering ethics training

First, the commitment of top management to ethics training is an essential condition for offering such training. The values of the corporation—and this implies in many firms the ethical assumptions of the CEO—will be the focus of discussion. In this respect, ethics training differs from technical and management training. The ethical assumptions that underlie the content of most other types of training are seldom explored systematically. For these reasons, management's general commitment to training should not be assumed to cover ethics training. A specific commitment is needed.

Second, the key issues of ethical importance in the organization must be identified in order to design an ethics training course that is relevant to the experience and needs of employees and managers. There are some ethical issues associated with the handling of information and data that are important to most organizations and others that are relevant only to a specific department within an organization. Suggestions on these will be offered later in the chapter.

Third, the trainer must have both an academic knowledge of ethics and an understanding of the management practice or of the specific technology—engineering, accounting, and so on. Team teaching if often used to achieve this combination.

Fourth, time is needed up front to gain support for an ethics training program. In some corporations gaining support is difficult enough for just the garden variety of management training, to say nothing of ethics training. Managers generally accept the value of improving their managerial skills. However, they may not be so open to the suggestion that they could improve their discrimination about what's right and wrong.

Orientation

Trainers in corporations are under pressure to design courses that are relevant to the needs and experience of the course participant. I'll offer some general observations about ethics training and, in the next section, a list of specific issues.

As far as possible, the selection of the ethical issues for discussion should focus on the areas for which the individuals in the seminar have some formal responsibility. In general, the greater the discretion a manager has, the greater are his or her ethical responsibilities. This is, of course, also true for employees with no managerial responsibilities. For example, accurate bookkeeping and the confidentiality of customer accounts are important to a bank. Although bookkeeping procedures and audits offer little discretion, the confidentiality of accounts is dependent on the integrity of employees.

A clear distinction should be maintained, too, between an open and free discussion about the ethical implications of an issue and what current corporate policies may be on that issue. There is nothing wrong with discussing corporate policy. Dilemmas that involve issues fundamental to a corporation's abilities to do business, such as those involving the integrity of a drug company's R&D operations, will be relevant and offer good material for an ethics seminar. A discussion of how actual management practices mirror the corporation's code of ethics may be the basis for a good discussion. But an indoctrination on the corporation's code of ethics alone should not be considered ethics training.

By the same token, ethics training should not be a gripe session for airing employee grievances. Certainly, the rights of employees may be legimate aspects of an ethical issue. But so are their responsibilities.

Ethical theory should be explained at relevant points in the discussions. Ethical theories, like the theories in any field, are the tools for thinking about problems. Ethics has a long history, and there is a rich body of ethical thought available. In general, the field is divided into meta-ethics and normative ethics. Meta-ethics analyzes the meaning of the terms used in ethical or moral arguments. Normative ethics focuses on the arguments used to defend or attack specific behaviors as being good or bad. Subfields of normative ethics include applied ethics and professional ethics. These examine the choices to be made in actual ethical dilemmas people face.

Applied ethics is often taught using case studies of real-life situations to stimulate students' ethical imagination. For example, the case studies might involve the following issues: Does a firm have a responsibility to provide day-care centers for working women in order to promote equal employment opportunity? Under what conditions, if any, is whistle blowing ethically responsible? Does the company have the right to require employees to take personality tests, polygraph examinations, or other tests that constitute, in the opinion of the employee, an invasion of privacy?

Starting with a case study that relates to the students' work situation is perhaps the best way to begin an ethics seminar. It gets people involved. And often, to their surprise, it exposes them to their peers' interpretations—defended as common sense—that differ from their own. The students' discovery that common sense doesn't carry them very far in achieving agreement in ethical dilemmas leads them to experience a need for more careful analysis. This need creates an appreciation for the rules of sound arguments—defining terms, the rules of relevance, generalization, and consequences. Meta-ethics and normative ethics, harnessed by consistent argument, are tools for analyzing ethical dilemmas.

There are issues of normative ethics—such as those involved in individual responsibility, honesty, and fairness—that are relevant to all employees. Gratuities and variable pricing are applied ethical issues in sales. Product safety is a concern in R&D.

It is difficult to keep a discussion of an ethical dilemma confined to the limits of functional areas such as sales or R&D. Soon, social and psychological considerations or questions about what really constitutes a fact arise. A brief review of what constitutes an ethical issue will help explain why this happens.

To say someone has acted ethically or unethically is to claim that the following four conditions exist:

1. You know the facts about the act, conduct, or behavior. However, facts come in all sizes and shapes in the worlds of physical science, statistical significance, professional judgments, and subjective experience.
2. The person had a choice of acting differently. However, perceiving choice is a learned activity that is strongly influenced by upbringing, training, and disposition.
3. The act or behavior conformed to or was in conflict with an ethical principle. For example, people should not be unnecessarily hurt or treated unfairly. But does this mean not hurt absolutely? And if not, then what criterion of degree applies?
4. The parties involved in the behavior are equivalent in some meaningful way relevant to ethical evaluations. For example, adults and children often are not considered equivalent in terms of responsibility. The pay differentials that exist between male and female workers often indicate they are not considered equivalent. And if they are not, how is this defended?

Under the guidance of a skilled leader, discussions will not degenerate into a quagmire of complexity. However, as in all new learning enterprises, students frequently have an initial feeling of buoyant enlightenment followed by deflation. The issues are more entangled than expected. A sense of confidence then develops as a conceptual road map of the issues becomes apparent.

A recurring criticism leveled at ethics training is that instructors often do not state their position at the conclusion of a discussion of an ethical dilemma. This may leave students with the impression that the issues of right and wrong are relative—it just depends on which ethical theory you wish to ride. In my opinion, this is as bad as running a corporate training program without taking a position on what constitutes effective management—implying that there are no practical differences among the ideas of Hertzberg, Machiavelli, and Chris Argyris.

To be sure, some ethical dilemmas are not easily or confidently resolved. However, there is broad agreement in our society on some elemental ethical principles. This agreement has been documented in survey after survey. In an unpublished 1981 American Management Associations' "Values and Expectations Survey" conducted throughout industry, being "honest" and "responsible" were chosen as the most admired traits of managers and subordinates by 87.7 percent and 88 percent, respectively, of managers responding to the survey. Being "capable" was a distant second, with 56 percent, followed by being "imaginative" (54.2 percent) and "logical" (49 percent). When there is a harmony between the standards of an organization and the standards employees aspire to, a consensual dynamic emerges, and enforcing corporate policy becomes a distant concern. This consensual agreement is a fulcrum point for managing corporate atmosphere.

Selecting the issues

This section offers three approaches for selecting issues pertinent to ethics training. First, we will take a look at a comprehensive list of issues that are important to modern corporate life and at the results of a survey which indicates the relative importance of various ethical issues to the firms studied. This provides a perspective on what others have considered important. Second, we will review a set of questions as a way of testing the relevance of various ethical issues. Finally, we will examine three common assumptions made in discussions about ethical dilemmas. . . .

Testing the relevance of ethical issues   Table 1 ranks the 51 ethical concerns most frequently mentioned in the codes of ethics of the 33 California corporations and the 281 Standard and Poor firms sampled in a California Roundtable survey. When the data in Table 1 are distributed by industrial grouping, the priority of the variables changes for some industries. The distribution of the variables is generally similar to the results of other surveys of corporate codes of ethics. An analysis of the variables in the table shows the importance of certain themes. For example, the theme of extortion, gifts, and kickbacks recurs in variables 1, 8, 14, 19, and 49, for a cumulative total percentage of 151.9. The themes of conflict of interest and insider information in variable 2, 5 and 27 have a total percentage of 121. The theme of honest record keeping appears in variables 9, 10, and 28 for a total percentage of 75.

Designing a course or seminar on ethics involves identifying the key issues around which the course will be developed. These, as mentioned, should be relevant to the participants and important to the organization. The following ten questions can be used to test the relevance of each of the issues listed in Table 1:

1. Do you think the issue is important to the maintenance or improvement of the corporate atmosphere?
2. Has the issue been mentioned in talks or papers given or issued by the CEO or a member of the board of directors?
3. Is there a corporate policy that clearly addresses this issue? And has it been consistently enforced?
4. Although there may be no formal policy, is there an understanding on the issue? What is it?
5. Have there been either grievances or instances in which this was raised as an issue?
6. Has the issue surfaced in exit interviews, performance evaluations, quality circle discussions, or suggestion boxes?
7. Has the question surfaced as a issue in management meetings?
8. Have shareholders' resolutions on the issue been voted on at the annual board of directors' meeting?
9. Is the issued addressed in federal or state legislation?
10. Could you develop a good case study on the issue that would stimulate seminar participants to examine their own attitudes and practices?

Common assumptions   There are several common assumptions about ethics that repeatedly surface in ethics courses. Being prepared to deal with these assumptions will facilitate a reasonable exploration of the selected issues.

To begin with, many people assume that what is legal is ethical or what is ethical is legal. These assumptions are reinforced by many corporate policies—entitled codes of ethics—that merely explain the importance of adhering to the law.

My own experience in conducting management training in high-technology corporations corresponds with Robert J. Baum's observations about engineering students:

Most engineering students assume that ethical knowledge is value-laden and totally "subjective," connected only to personal intuitions belonging to individual persons. Most of them also assume that science is concerned with factual knowledge about the external world and thus is totally objective. Since ethical knowledge is subjective and based on internal intuitions of individual persons, they believe that there is no basis whatsoever for resolving disagreements among individuals concerning ethical matters.

A thoroughgoing ethical relativism is therefore a common starting point for many engineering students at the beginning of an ethics course. But paradoxically, many engineering students are ethical absolutists, although they also share the relativists' assumptions that there is no rational basis for comparing ethical positions, and they are unwilling (and/or unable) to present any arguments in defense of their own principles.

They simply assert that they are true absolutely and apply to all individuals (not just themselves). At best, their position can be characterized as one of "naive intuitionism."[6]

The acceptance of what you cannot change is often cited as a step toward wisdom. Some people also feel that if there is nothing you can do to prevent an unethical act from occurring, you have no responsibility to take a stand on the issue. This outlook is reinforced in organizations where the division of management responsibilities is sharply defined. The perspective people develop about their chances for success or failure become self-fulfilling prophecies. This is probably the most powerful factor in motivation as defined by self-actualization. It's also a powerful factor in shaping people's concept of responsibility.

Instructional strategies

The design, organization, and conduct of an ethics course can be handled in much the same way as leadership training. Case studies, lecturettes, group discussions and exercises, and assigned readings can be used. Just as some management trainees have difficulty accepting the value of a leadership style that is different from their own pattern, some people do not see that an ethical dilemma can be evaluated from a perspective that varies from their own.

The evaluation of corporate training programs is a continuing concern. How are the benefits of training established so the costs can be justified? The limitations on supervisory leadership courses and the opportunities for evaluating such courses also apply to ethics training. A large body of literature covering training evaluation is available.

There are some differences worth noting between management training and ethics training. First, ethics training challenges people to consider their behavior at a more fundamental level than does management training. People do feel that personal integrity is more important than being an effective manager.

Second, more of management training can be related to people's experiences than is usually possible in ethics training. Ethical theory depends more on abstract thinking than management training, which is grounded in behavioral research or established routines like accounting. Some people have difficulty making the transition from a concept to its practical application. This is why it is so important to choose ethical issues that relate as closely as possible to people's work situations.

One way to relate theory to practice is to have the seminar participants develop their own case studies of ethical dilemmas. Not only does this offer a practical exercise, but it will generate relevant case studies to be exchanged with others in the class for evaluation

and problem solving. With a little encouragement, course participants should be able to draw from their own experiences to develop
such case studies.

The following is a typical case study that illustrates the tension
between two seemingly reasonable interests—John's desire to "restore some peace in the family" and "company policy" on expense
accounts:

John Voyage is the national sales manager for Runabout Motorcycles, an
English firm attempting to establish operations in the United States.
Since John is the only fully-trained salesman, he needs to give continual
assistance to his men in the field. In the past year, he had been on the
road two or three days every week. His wife has started to complain and
does not seem to understand his position. In order to restore some peace
to the family, John has started taking his wife with him whenever he
travels to any point of interest. Since he approves his own expenses for
accounting, he bills the company for some of his wife's expenses, though
this is against company policy. He tries to keep the overall bill to the
company within reasonable limits by taking a double room at a slightly
less expensive hotel, and by flying tourist instead of first class. Frequently the bill he puts in is no higher than it would have been if he were
traveling alone.

John argues that the company policy does not really apply to a case
like his. Moreover, he feels the company ought to be willing to help him
in keeping his family intact.[7]

Besides being expected to offer a solution for how the issue
might be resolved, class participants are expected to be able to identify the types of reasoning or ethical assumptions John is using and
whether these are consistent. And if not, how would the inconsisten-
cies be described?

Summary

There is a growing awareness among thoughtful managers that the
key to more effective direction and control of the corporate atmosphere lies in developing norms that can be consistently reinforced.
Furthermore, many corporations have excellent codes of ethics that
encourage employees to rely on their own sense of values. These new
developments are creating a climate that makes ethics training possible. Opportunities exist in every corporation to offer relevant
training that will capture the imagination of participants and benefit the organization.

The atmosphere of an organization can be managed success-
fully if executives establish goals and management systems that are
compatible with their philosophy. A management philosophy that
consistently accommodates the needs of both management and employees will increase a manager's chances of effective control as well
as promote productivity. The need to have top management and

middle managers with the capacity to handle ethical problems and to direct a corporation with an eye to its atmosphere will increase. This will be true for several reasons that go beyond the issues already discussed in this chapter.

First, the issue of "fair share" will be of increasing concern to employees and the public in the future because the growth rate of our economy has slowed. In a booming economy where everyone's income is rising, even though it may be rising at different rates, people are less concerned about what others make. This is true in the corporation and true in the public sector. The capacity of the federal government to maintain the current relative stability of income distribution in this country is being undermined by this slowing economy. For example, the average income of the fastest-growing group in the United States, the aged, is equal to the average income of all groups. However, if Social Security and other transfer payments such as Medicaid and Medicare were removed, the average income of the aged would be cut by 50 percent.

Second, international trade is forcing managers to come to terms with the difficult cultural conflicts that stand in the way of smooth trade relationships. Bribery by foreign nationals is the story line in the Abscam theater. But this is only one issue. The United Nations has established a charter of economic issues and duties of states. The International Chamber of Commerce has established guidelines for international investments. Throughout these international guidelines runs a consistent theme of establishing equivalent positions. This is, of course, a basic condition for a dignified and ethical relationship.

Third, companies engaged in government work must now negotiate with the government under the rules of the Freedom of Information Act as to what is proprietary information and what is legally public information. In this process, the issue of what is an honest or necessary disclosure is being critically reevaluated. Also, the increased use of computers by government and business is raising many questions about corporate disclosure.

Clearly, the pressures on our society and businesses are continuing. It is becoming more and more important to restabilize important relationships we all experience. The place of work is one of the most common denominators. Over four-fifths of the labor force works in the private sector. Therefore, business has an enormous opportunity to help restabilize our society. Ethics training can play a central role in this process.

Notes

1. *BankAmerica Corporation Code of Corporate Conduct*, May 12, 1978, p. 1.

2. M.R. Cooper, B. Morgan, P.M. Foley, and L.B. Kaplan, "Changing Employee Values: Deepening Discon-

tent?" *Harvard Business Review* (January 1979), p. 124.

3. Daniel Callahan and Sissela Bok, project directors, *The Teaching of Ethics in Higher Education,* a report by the Hastings Center (Hastings-on-Hudson, N.Y.: The Hastings Center, 1980), p. 48.

4. Terrence E. Deal and Allen A. Kennedy, *Corporate Cultures: The Rights and Rituals of Corporate Life* (Reading, Mass.: Addison-Wesley, 1982), Part I, pp. 3–85.

5. William Goode, *The Celebration of Heroes: Prestige as a Control System* (Berkeley: University of California Press, 1978), p. 298.

6. *Ethics and Engineering Curricula,* a report for the Hastings Center (Hastings-on-Hudson, N.Y.: The Hastings Center, 1980), p. 12.

7. Thomas M. Garrett et al., *Cases in Business Ethics* (Englewood Cliffs, N.J.: Prentice-Hall, 1968), p. 13.

PART 4

Ethical Codes: Principles and Practice

The Problem of Moral Reasoning in Public Administration: The Case for a Code of Ethics

Ralph Clark Chandler

Arguments against a code of ethics

The first argument against a code of ethics is that we should resist moralizing as a practical matter. We live in the residue of the implicit but clearly understood American tradition that liberty is the first principle of the republic, with prosperity close behind. If the framers had allowed the Presbyterians to take us too far into a discussion of the public good, the result would probably have been the kind of regimentation, ordering, and indoctrination that might have worked in Geneva and the Massachusetts Bay Colony, but was not preferred in New York and Virginia. Theocracy was out, not because the framers were immoral, but because a self-consciously moral society would have to put duties first and relegate rights and everything else that is private to a subordinate place in the life of the republic. It was clear to Publius in *The Federalist*, as well as in the debates of the Constitutional Convention, that political liberty and economic energy unavoidably engender some immorality, but that government can control it without the institutional consequences of preaching and being preached to. The tradition of American public administration came to be that we ought to live with a moderate degree of immorality and condemn the self-righteous moralist who forgets that men and women were not angels. The tradition has served us well.[1]

Another reason some of us are less than enthusiastic about a code of ethics is that our pathfinders periodically celebrate the unique virtues of consensus building and proceduralism in American society. By this line of reasoning, the lack of stated public purpose is one of the nation's fundamental strengths, because throughout our national history continuing redefinitions of purpose and compromise of principle have allowed us to make the incremental changes necessary for political stability. They have also permitted us to flourish at once as a republic and as an empire, as a constitutionally limited federal state governed by law and as an unlimited unitary state with expanded economic and territorial ambitions. Proceduralism is necessary because in a pluralist pressure system an article of faith must be that from the clash of opposites, contraries, extremes, and poles will come not the victory of any one, but the mediation and accommodation of all. Truth, unity, and especially morality can never be forged from one ideal form. They must be hammered out on the anvil of debate. Thus necessity has become a virtue in public administration, and consensus is built around the agreement to agree on nothing substantive. Assent is given not to value, but to value default. The irony of the proceduralist position, of course, is that as the need for shared values in an increasingly factionalized and anomic society grows, adversaries who no longer find in their disagreements a basis for common norms are transformed from adversaries into enemies.[2]

A third reason which helps to explain our discomfort with a code of ethics is the lingering influence of both Woodrow Wilson and Max Weber. Wilson maintained that administration stands apart "even from the debatable ground of constitutional study. It is part of political life only as the methods of the countinghouse are a part of the life of society; only as machinery is part of the manufactured product."[3] It follows that where there is no discretion there is no moral responsibility. Weber also spoke of "the bureaucratic machine" in which the honor of the civil servant is vested in his or her ability to execute conscientiously the order of superior authorities, "exactly as if the order agreed with his own conviction. This holds even if the order appears wrong to him, and if, despite the civil servant's remonstrances, the authority insists on the order. Without *this moral discipline* [emphasis added] and self-denial, in the highest sense, the whole apparatus would fall to pieces."[4] Thus Weber's administrator considers it moral to avoid morality, with the result that the organization in which he or she serves becomes incapable of determining how its power should be used. The organization schools itself in moral illiteracy and the administrator becomes the victim of his or her own success. This is the condition Erich Fromm describes as the state of moral confusion where man is left without the guidance of either revelation or reason. The result is the acceptance of a relativistic position which proposes that value judgments and ethical norms are exclusively matters of taste or arbitrary preference and that no objectively valid moral statement can be made.[5]

There are many other arguments against a code of ethics. Although some of us would be uncomfortable with the comparison, a large number of American public administrators agree with the prophet Jeremiah that the laws of right behavior are written on one's heart, not on paper. Others think that professional organizations such as the American Society for Public Administration (ASPA) are too diverse for a code to apply to all parts of it, and that, since an ethics code is largely unenforceable anyway, we should not have one. Still others resist what they call the overly moralistic and preachy language of ethics codes in general, which raises for these critics the specter of the profession caving in to the moral majority.

Arguments for a code of ethics

The first argument *for* a code might be called the argument from objectivism. To take objectivism seriously, however, or indeed to take seriously any of the affirmative arguments, one probably must agree with Wallace S. Sayre that administrative discourse at any level of sophistication frequently resolves itself into problems of political theory. This is a difficult saying for pluralists and proceduralists, because they tend to take as an article of faith that the *process* of arriving at consensus is ultimately more important than both theory and the substance of any words agreed upon. Nevertheless, as long as the letterhead of the American Society for Public Administration says it exists to advance the science and art, as well as the processes, of public administration, the analysis of thought and language becomes more than a frivolous exercise.

Objectivism refers to the ancient debate in philosophy about transcendent values. It posits a center of value external to human collectivities and is represented in such concepts as God, the Good, and in Paul Tillich's phrase "the ultimate ground of being." In a code of ethics it typically is reflected in such phrases as "public morality," "the sovereignty of the people," and in references to *the* law. Objectivism is best understood in comparison to its opposite, subjectivism, which holds that the center of value is somewhere in the human condition. Subjectivism is represented in such concepts as humanism, happiness, and "the dignity of man." In public administration it is thoroughgoing in Simmons and Dvorin's concept of radical humanism. Subjectivists tend to reject "public morality," for example, as a self-contradictory term. They translate "the sovereignty of the people" into "the best interests of the public," and they change *the* law, which has no objective existence, into *laws*, which are culturally determined. Thus morally transcendent ideas become ethically relative ones.

Objectivists maintain that ontological ethics invite the administrator to be ethical, because they encourage him or her to make choices and judgments and to pursue actions. Actions are the predicates of being. Unless one assumes the risks attendant on them, he or she vacates the ethical arena. Objectivist codes therefore frequently employ active transitive verbs rather than intransitive verbs of being. Note the verbs "fight," "revere," "obey," "incite," "strive," "quicken," and "transmit" in one of the best-known of the objectivist codes.

The Athenian oath

We will never bring disgrace to this our city
by any act of dishonesty or cowardice,
nor ever desert our suffering comrades in the ranks;

We will fight for the ideals and the sacred things of the city,
both alone and with many;

We will revere and obey the city's laws and
do our best to incite to a like respect and reverence
those who are prone to annul or set them at naught;

We will strive unceasingly to quicken
the public sense of public duty;

That thus, in all these ways, we will transmit this city
not only not less, but greater, better and more beautiful
than it was transmitted to us.

The Athenian Oath also illustrates the second argument for a code of ethics. It is the argument from community. In this view, moral behavior in public administration is not just a matter of private preferences and personal integrity. The determination of what is a gift and what is a bribe rests with the giver as well as the receiver. Judgments about right and wrong are community decisions as well as private ones. The community is the arbiter of what is ethical. The communal "we," with its varied implications of personalized ownership, is strikingly apparent in the Athenian Oath and in other codes. Aristotle warned repeatedly that it is possible to obey laws and regulations and still be unethical. The community looks at the nature of an act in order to decide whether it is moral or not. Stephen K. Bailey wrote: "There is not a moral vice which cannot be made into relative good by context. There is not a moral virtue which cannot in peculiar circumstances have patently evil results."[6] Laws govern all actions of the public service, but it is equally true that actors govern. Laws regulate people, not action, and people are part of a community. They are not islands unto themselves.

Vincent Ostrom has written that any normal science needs general agreement about a basic theoretical paradigm or framework in which "a community of scholars shares common theoretical assumptions, and a common language defining essential terms and relationships."[7] Proponents of a code argue that the self-interestedness of relativism represents a loss of paradigm, and with it a loss of a sense of community. There cannot be a paradigm without a community.

A third argument advanced for a code of ethics is the argument from courage. G. K. Chesterton once remarked that where there is no courage, there is no room for any other virtue. Courage holds up idealism in a field where the practice of *realpolitik* reflects our true learnings that human life is characterized by a little more or a little less justice, and a little more or a little less equity. Theologian Rheinhold Neibuhr has told us why impossible ideals are nevertheless relevant: they function prophetically. They demand the best, while they expose "the impotence and corruption of human nature." Sin-talk is admittedly old-fashioned, restrictive, and somewhat embarrassing, but if this is the only reason that the parlance of idealism is rejected, we also put ourselves out of touch with a rich classical tradition which sought for moral unity and a higher law in conversation that has little to do with sin.

The argument from courage maintains that the criticism of public administration as being amoral is validated in anti-code sentiment. The politics-administration dichotomy appears to be alive and well, despite Nicholas Henry's hope that the public administrator is now forced to make decisions "not on the comfortable basis of efficiency, economy, and administrative principles, but on the more agonizing criteria of morality as well."[8] The collection of anti-code opinions we have variously described as relativistic, proceduralist, and pluralist certainly does not agonize very much. Rather than agonize, it resorts to neutralized language, as when the condemnation of waste and abuse of government funds is transformed into the affirmation of efficient and effective management.

Henry notes that the counter-culture's charge of administrative amorality is essentially a linguistic one. "It holds that the symbols and values of technological society prevent individual men and women from choosing."[9] When the American Institute of Planners surveyed 1,178 planners in 1979, for example, to determine "what planners think is ethical and why," it discovered that professionals who considered themselves "technicians" indicated they were value-neutral 81 percent of the time.[10]

The avoidance of choice affirms the administrator as technician. In its educational dimension, it refuses responsibility for socializing new professionals in a broader view of the science and art of public administration. It pretends once again that public administrators do in fact strictly adhere to value-free decision making. Idealists say further that opposition to the language of ethical choice in a code extends the widespread misunderstanding of what "moral" means. It has become a pejorative term in many circles, probably aggravated by the moral majority movement. It connotes judgment, condemnation, narrow-mindedness, obsessive or compulsive religion, and legalism. "Moral" does indeed involve standards of conduct, but these standards are as much voluntarily assumed as they are enjoined from without. Once assumed, however, the standards do impose obligations of choice, and they withdraw certain areas of conduct from the free option of the individual to do as he or she pleases. That must be the problem.

Further analysis of the positions

There is something persuasive in each of these contending positions: the arguments against a code of ethics from practicality, procedure, and administrative theory, and the arguments for a code of ethics from objectivism, community, and courage. Further analysis of the positions suggests nuances of meaning that have important ramifications for the society as a whole. Let us begin where the *anti* statements begin, and that is with history.

The negative argument from practicality   It is true that the founders counseled moderation on moral matters. They said that unbounded moralism is as self-indulgent as any other form of excess. If there was a need for government to control the abuses following from selfishness, given the observed fact that the basic motivation of people is self-interest, there was an equal need to insist that acts of government control ought also to be bounded. The founders were widely acclaimed for such insights into human nature, and for the countervailing instrumentalities of government they devised.

Consider, however, the following conundrum in logic and in historical practice. When James Madison pointed out in *The Federalist* that men, and presumably women, are not angels, he also noted that if they were, no government would be necessary. That meant at the time that government was necessary, and that the Constitution should be ratified. Since government is administered, however, by the same men and women who are not angels, where is Madison's argument if the instrumentalities of government are themselves corrupt? He and other moderates rested their case, after all, on the fact that government can keep public immorality within reasonable bounds.

The problem is that the historical record sustains the view that corruption is endemic in the American political and administrative system and that it constantly assaults reasonable bounds. From the Yazoo land fraud in the 1790s, to the bribery of members of Congress by officials of the Second United States Bank in the 1830s, to the scandals surrounding Union Pacific Railroad land acquisitions in the 1870s, to Teapot Dome and Elk Hills in the 1920s, to the revelations of kickbacks in tax settlements by collectors of internal

revenue in the 1950s, to the Vietnam order of battle misrepresenta-
tions in the 1960s, to the Watergate phenomenon in the 1970s, to
ABSCAM in the early 1980s, and many other instances in between,
our history can be read as a litany of lies, avarice, and greed. In
Capitalism the Creator, historian Carl Snyder calls the characteristics of the sharp dealer the great force in the building of America.

In addition, consider the opinion of Henry Steele Commager. In
"A Historian Looks at Our Political Morality," he discusses the presuppositions of certain national policy decisions. These had to do
with our collective responsibility for what he describes as "the con-
quest and decimation of the Indian," slavery defended as a moral
good, the child labor of the industrial revolution explained as the
necessary price of progress, and the Vietnam War pursued as the
logical result of "better dead than Red." Commager concluded that
despite the hopes of Madison, the instrumentalities of government
cannot in fact control immorality.

Carl Sandburg in his role of poet as well as historian had a
kinder indictment of those burdened with the exigencies of ethical
choice. He said we are all liars, just different kinds.

People lie because they don't remember
clear what they say.

People lie because they can't help
making a story better than it was
the way it happened.

People tell white lies so as to be decent
to others.

People lie in a pinch, hating to do it,
but lying on because it might be worse.

And people lie just to be liars
for crooked gain.

What sort of liar are you?

Which of these liars are you?

Perhaps we are the kind of liar Alexander Hamilton was. In
trying to help Madison deal with the problem of corrupt human nature, he wrote:

The aim of every political constitution is, or ought to be, first to obtain
for rulers men who possess most wisdom to discern, and most virtue to
pursue, the common good of society; and in the next place *to take the most
effectual precautions for keeping them virtuous* [emphasis added].

The ink was hardly dry on this issue of *The Federalist* when the
Yazoo land fraud case came to light. The state of Georgia, its legislature bribed by New England financiers, sold to private speculators
most of what is today the states of Alabama and Mississippi at one
and one-half cents an acre. Involved in the graft were two United

States Senators, including Robert Morris of Pennsylvania, two Congressmen, three leading jurists, including Associate Supreme Court Justice James Wilson, and assorted civil servants who could have stopped the scheme at almost any point in its development, but remained neutral.

The story is celebrated and involved and eventually resulted in a major Supreme Court decision, *Fletcher v. Peck* (1810). The speculators won out finally because the Marshall Court held invalid an act of a subsequent Georgia legislature repealing the sale. The bribers kept their profits largely through the efforts of their sagacious lawyer, the same Alexander Hamilton who had called for effectual precautions for keeping public officials virtuous.[11]

The negative argument from procedure   As long as the United States was a land of plenty and had a manifest destiny, the nation was like a good centerfielder. It could outrun many of its mistakes as long as there was expansion room and abundance. Never mind Nicholas Biddle's bribe of Daniel Webster, Henry Clay, John C. Calhoun, and 52 other members of Congress in exchange for the renewal of the charter of the Second United States Bank in 1833.[12] Such shenanigans were an aspect of the ethos of privatism, material ambition, and self-sufficiency, shielded as they were by the rhetoric of personal and national independence.

That rhetoric sounds hollow in the 1980s, however. The opposites of independence, interdependence and cooperation, were once considered weaknesses of the American national character, but now they are necessities. They spring from a sense of common limits. In the old rhetoric, words, like everything else, could be wasted as long as open spaces, empty jobs, and unmade fortunes were the conditions of American life. Now the nation is faced with the prospect of limited growth, scarce resources, and the bankruptcy of privatism. Just as abundance was the natural soil of competitive individualism, scarcity is the soil of mutualism. In scarcity and mutuality words are important. They may not change behavior, but they do other essential things in a circumscribed environment where the vision of administrators is crucial to survival: they inspire, they set a tone, and they create expectations. They provide points of reference for living in the settled land. If proceduralists throw away the words of idealism, perhaps in ignorance of what they mean, they will deprive themselves of a singular source of power in understanding and manipulating the new conditions of American life.

The dilemma of faith in proceduralism and countervailing power versus the requirements of careful talk in mutualism invites more authoritative solutions than those immediately discoverable in the more patient processes of moral reasoning. The classical culture Publius and other founders admired provides the following example of the problem. By the year A.D. 284 the Roman administrative class felt itself so undermined by Christian talk about unselfishness and moral responsibility that it undertook to support Diocletian as a candidate for Emperor of the Roman Empire. He was the person most likely to restore the old glory. The wellsprings of that were understood as the proper administration of Rome's vast and still largely undiminished resources. It is true that Diocletian was only half civilized, but he was a professional soldier who believed in consensus, citizen responsibility, restraint, and especially practicality. As emperor he enforced fixed prices to fight inflation. He allowed the patrician class to make money, explaining that some of it would trickle down to the plebeians. He spent millions on national defense. In addition, he cut welfare programs. He also persecuted the Christians. But 20 years later Diocletian abdicated in despair. He retired to a palace built like a fortress in what is today Yugoslavia, and spent the rest of his life raising vegetables. Neither he nor the administrative class who desperately pursued rectitude by honoring the old ways ever really understood how Rome had changed, and how the consensus-building procedures of the old ways were irrelevant for the new.

Constantine did understand, however. Within 20 years of Diocletian's abdication, he had established the Constantinian Settlement, which was not much more than official recognition of Christian idealism as symbolically useful for the new conditions of Roman life. Its language of heroism, transcendence, and mutualism gave rise to a new kind of civilization that would last a thousand years. Constantine admitted that the *Pax Romana* could no longer be imposed. He said that unlimited national power was a myth. He forced the administrative class to acknowledge that it had both discretionary power and the moral responsibility which went with it. This simple reorientation released remarkable new energies in Roman life.

The negative argument from administrative theory   The anti-code argument from practicality is unconvincing because government cannot control immorality. The anti-code argument from procedure is something of an anachronism because it is out of sync with the changing and changed conditions of American life. The anti-code argument from administrative theory is flawed because the administrative man or woman it posits never really existed and cannot exist psychologically except in the models built by Woodrow Wilson and Max Weber.

Weber's morally neutral administrator who claimed he was not responsible for the crimes of German National Socialism in the 1930s and 1940s, for example, was told at the Nuremberg trials that he was responsible. Wilson's administrative technician who says he cannot seek personal goals within the organization has found himself increasingly a victim of bureaupathology as he therefore attaches himself ritualistically to routines and procedures. He attempts to deny human characteristics which will not be denied.

Administrative theorists such as Michel Crozier and Victor A. Thompson have pointed out that there is no necessary correlation between bureaucracy as a rational system and the irrational behavior of the body of civil servants who are the instrumentalities of government. Civil servants are frequently observed as being aloof, bored, negative, inefficient, impolite, unhelpful, and abusers of the power that official doctrine says they do not have. Thompson says such bureaupathetic behavior is exhibited by people who interpret any challenge to existing rules as a threat to their own security. Robert K. Merton adds that the tendency of bureaucracies to adhere to rules as ends in themselves, which he calls goal displacement, results in a process of sanctification in which bureaucratic procedures are invested with attitudes of moral legitimacy. Procedures are established as values in their own right, and are no longer viewed as merely technical means for expediting administration. Sentiments of devotion to the methodical performance of routine activities are more intense than is technically necessary. Thus instrumental values become terminal values.[13]

The reader will note such words as "ritualistically," "doctrine," "sanctification," "moral legitimacy," and "sentiments of devotion" in the foregoing description. These and similar words appear more and more frequently in modern administrative analysis. They are value-laden and even religious in their affect. One must ask, therefore, if "value neutral" civil servants can pass through a "process of sanctification" to make their enterprises "morally legitimate" (even if bureaupathetic), why can they not also embrace processes of moral reasoning which would produce professional standards from outside the limitations of their organizations and their psyches. White magic may be as good as black magic.

More directly in answer to Wilson and Weber and their modern disciples is the apparent fact that most public policy has as its declared aim some public good. Normative forces in the political order shaped the policy. The moral dimensions of policy warrant, and perhaps demand, examination by those who will execute it. Fleishman and Payne have listed the reasons: (1) the duty of the public official may be unclear because of conflicting obligations or because of conflict between an obligation and legitimate self-interest; (2) the values embodied in policy options may be disputed or insufficiently understood; and, (3) the normative principles guiding policy are themselves frequently unclear or contradictory.[14]

Whatever the doctrine of value neutrality may state, the real decisions of public officials frequently involve ethical choices and resolution of ethical dilemmas. Administrators choose daily between and among conflicting values in the interpretation of the ultimate goals of policy. Neither legislatures nor courts offer definitive interpretations of the vast majority of issues which arise administratively. Administrators must delineate the law. Their policies, programs, instructions, rules, procedures, and day-to-day decisions may not always agree with the intent of the elected officials who broadly structured the law in the first place, or with the courts who are too busy to define it. Many administrators live in a no-man's-land of what is lawful, what is wise, and what is in the public interest. The real question is not whether they inhabit the land of moral ambiguity, but how well equipped they are to survive in it without seeking refuge in bureaupathology. An enhanced and self-consciously developed capacity to engage in moral reasoning, and even an occasional glance at a modern version of the Athenian Oath, might help.

The affirmative argument from objectivism   The affirmation of transcendent values moves to correct the conditions of Hannah Arendt's remark that authority has vanished in modern society. Statements of objective truth help reduce the moral confusion which the lack of authority brings. Aristotle said we do not do good acts because we are already good, the precise position of the founders of the American republic; we do good acts because they have been prescribed by the requirements of virtue, good manners, the revealed word of God, tradition, the elders, the common law, the Constitution, or some other source of transcendent authority; and in the process of doing good acts, we become good. Aristotle may have been the first behaviorist.

Authority has had a difficult time in ethical theory since the Reformation. Before the Reformation the Christian West was a monolith of values, authority, and the affirmation of objective truth. There were definitive provisions for the resolution of any ethical dispute. The Reformation shattered that sense of certainty with Martin Luther's doctrine of the priesthood of all believers. Competing orthodoxies emerged, and individuals came to believe they were their own mediators of religious and moral truth. John Calvin added to Luther's doctrine that God alone was the Lord of the conscience, and the idea of moral autonomy was born.

It has been a heavy burden to bear. One wonders if Luther and Calvin would have been quite so definite about individualism if they had understood the implications of the work of Copernicus. His calculations dislodged man from his central place in creation and cast him adrift in a universe where there was no absolute point of reference. Later, Charles Darwin's *Origin of Species* did for anthropology what Copernicus had done for physics. Together they made man's place in nature an enigma. Mankind had to ask if the world were a number which came up in a cosmic Monte Carlo game. If man is not the product of divine intention, and if the earth evolved from blind chance, there cannot be moral certainty about anything.

The subsequent atomization of moral philosophy means it has significant disabilities to overcome if it is to respond to its current summons to deal with the ethical crisis of American culture. Among these disabilities are: (1) the language of moral discourse tends to be a collection of fragments of culturally dead large-scale philosophical systems, as when remnants of the medieval doctrine of the just war contend against truncated and secondhand versions of utilitarianism, and both of these are confronted in turn by amateur Machiavellianism; (2) the loss of the vision of the whole means ethics is constantly being rediscovered in American society, rather than being a permanent cultural enterprise, with the result being occasional statements of temporary and fragile moral premises about which there is little agreement and over which there are endless battles of assertion and counterassertion; (3) the inevitable appeal to intuition which moral philosophy must make faces the probability that the prephilosophical intuitions which evaluate the appeal are so dominated by what Alasdir MacIntyre calls "an unsystematic conceptual archaeology" that rational discourse on moral subjects is impossible in popular forums.

Meanwhile the ongoing celebration of moral autonomy helps to explain why the American Society for Public Administration cannot agree on a code of ethics. Gerald Dworkin says a person is morally autonomous if he or she: (1) defines his or her own moral principles; (2) engages his or her will or volition as the ultimate source of authority; (3) is involved in the decision regarding which moral principles are binding on him or her personally; (4) bears the responsibility for the moral theory he or she accepts and applies; and (5) refuses to accept external moral authority, except as independently filtered.

A moral theory which stresses autonomy will have difficulty with the central moral category of obligation. To be obliged is to be bound, and to be bound is to be restricted. If the individual is the primary moral agent, there cannot be a priori assumptions about the principles which oblige. It does not matter that they are aspects of a moral tradition passed on as part of one's training and/or professional standards, or that they are the principles of Gandhi, Thoreau, Socrates, Confucius, Tolstoy, or Jesus. The tyranny of the self is such that it must mediate all authority claiming to represent objective truth. Theologians used to call that original sin.

The affirmative argument from community   A good deal has been written about public administration's inability to define itself as a profession and as an academic discipline. Dwight Waldo's idea of the disparate elements of public administration forming a holding company remains the best analogy for what public administration really is. Yet a holding company by definition is able to control other companies by virtue of stock ownership in them. The companies together form a community held together by income derived from the exchange of stock and securities among themselves and with others.

The American Society for Public Administration cannot control even one of its members who may be convicted of fraud, embezzlement, or mismanagement of any kind. There is no legal tender, no commonly agreed-upon currency, the counterfeit of which is the legal basis for expulsion from the Society. The current by-laws provide no standards of professional behavior against which a member can be judged as unprofessional. Theoretically one could sit in prison in violation of fundamental professional norms and simultaneously maintain membership in ASPA, because the organization has never stated its norms in an enforceable code of ethics. Surely this condition militates against the coming of age of public administration in the United States. A community of any kind must have legal tender, not only to establish its own identity, but to gain the sanction of the larger community with which it does business. [In 1985, ASPA did adopt a Code of Ethics with implementation guidelines; as of 1988, however, no procedures for enforcement had been developed. Ed.]

The affirmative argument from courage   In his closing argument in the *Glavis-Ballinger* case of 1910, Justice Louis Brandeis provided the following vision of the public servant:

They cannot be worthy of the respect and admiration of the people unless they add to the virtue of obedience some other virtues—virtues of manliness, of truth, of courage, of willingness to risk position, of the willingness to risk criticism, of the willingness to risk the misunderstanding that so often comes when people do the heroic thing.[15]

The "heroic thing" puts us back in Athens among those who "revere," "strive," and "transmit," and it recalls those men and women who once pledged their lives, their fortunes, and their sacred honor to secure the blessings of liberty to the young American republic and its posterity. Psychologists tell us that accepting risks and assuming vulnerability are signs of health in a person or an organization. If we are life-affirming people, we do not merely tolerate our tasks from economic necessity, but we find beauty, meaning, and value in the tasks themselves, even if they are mundane administrative chores. Insofar as we find beauty in them, we find the elusive relationship between aesthetics and ethics that Plato said is the essence of the good life. Insofar as we find meaning and value in them, we also encounter moral choice and moral talk. Jean-Paul Sartre said that to avoid such talk and such choice is bad *faith*—an interesting choice of words for an atheist. Faith therefore is not merely a religious phenomenon. Faith is saying yes to life in the midst of its tragedies, ambiguities, and hard moral choices. Faith makes felicitous that which in any case is necessary.

Notes

1. See Robert A. Goldwin, "Of Men and Angels: A Search for Morality in the Constitution," in Robert H. Horwitz, ed., *The Moral Foundations of the American Republic*, second edition (Charlottesville: The University of Virginia Press, 1982), pp. 1-18.

2. See Benjamin R. Barber, "The Compromised Republic: Public Purposeless in America," in Horwitz, *op. cit.*, pp. 19-38.

3. Woodrow Wilson, "The Study of Administration," *Political Science Quarterly*, Vol. 11, No. 1 (June 1887), in Jay M. Shafritz and Albert C. Hyde (eds.), *Classics of Public Administration* (Oak Park, Ill.: Moore Publishing Company, 1978), p. 10.

4. Max Weber in H. H. Gerth and C. Wright Mills (eds.), *From Max Weber: Essays in Sociology* (New York: Oxford University Press, 1946), p. 95.

5. See Erich Fromm, *Man for Himself: An Inquiry into the Psychology of Ethics* (New York: Fawcett Book Group, 1978).

6. Stephen K. Bailey, quoted in Dwight Waldo, *The Enterprise of Public Administration* (Novato, Calif.: Chandler and Sharp Publishers, Inc., 1980), p. 99.

7. Vincent Ostrom, *The Intellectual Crisis in American Public Administration*, revised edition (University, Ala.: The University of Alabama Press, 1974), p. 13.

8. Nicholas Henry, *Public Administration and Public Affairs*, second edition (Englewood Cliffs, N.J.: Prentice-Hall, Inc., 1980), p. 132.

9. *Ibid.*, p. 134.

10. Elizabeth Howe and Jerome Kaufman, "The Ethics of Contemporary American Planners," *The APA Journal*, July 1979, pp. 243-254.

11. See Ralph Clark Chandler, "Ethics and Public Policy," *Commonweal*, Vol CV, No. 10 (May 12, 1978), pp. 302-309.

12. *Ibid.*, p. 304.

13. See Ralph Clark Chandler and Jack C. Plano, *The Public Administration Dictionary* (New York: John Wiley and Sons, 1982) for a discussion of bureaupathology, goal displacement, Neo-Weberism, and related ideas, especially pages 158-159, 173-174, and 195-196.

14. Fleishman, Joel L., and Payne, Bruce L., *Ethical Dilemmas and the Education of Policymakers* (Hastings-on-Hudson, N.Y.: The Hastings Institute, 1980), p. 15.

15. Quoted in J.D. Williams, *Public Administration: The People's Business* (Boston: Little, Brown and Company, 1980), p. 541.

Ethical Problems Today

Revan A. F. Tranter

The year was 1924. Lindbergh had yet to make his transatlantic flight. Churchill, in one of his wilderness periods, had just been defeated for a Parliamentary seat. The Australian Parliament had yet to move from Melbourne to Canberra, the new capital. Canada wasn't yet complete: Newfoundland was still a British colony. Hitler was in his jail cell writing *Mein Kampf.* Coolidge was President of the United States. Babe Ruth was in his element. And Perry Cookingham was yet to begin his career as a city manager.

It was, as they say, a different era in 1924, when ICMA's original Code of Ethics was published. As the Second Tenet put it: "No man should accept a position of City Manager unless he believes in the Council-Manager plan of Government." There were no assistants; no county administrators; no COG directors; no general management administrators; no members in Australia, Britain, or New Zealand; no consultants; and no women or minorities. Now we have them all. We also have two-career couples, public-private partnerships, and members with enough disposable income to invest in real estate.

To cope with these changes, the Code of Ethics has had to move with the times. It is now in its sixth edition (1976) and comes with Guidelines and Rules of Procedure for Enforcement. In 1987, the Executive Board approved a series of amendments to the Guidelines and the Rules of Procedure.

The amendments accomplish two things:

1. They bring the Guidelines (and therefore the Code) up to date by recognizing changes in our society and our profession.

Reprinted with permission from *Public Management* magazine (August 1987): 2–5.

2. They streamline the Rules of Procedure for Enforcement and
    at the same time improve the Rules' legal protection both for
    members and for the Association.

In spite of the changes made necessary by time, one thing has
remained constant. We have a Code of Ethics, not a Code of Law.
After all, we are a profession, and in making that claim we accept
and adhere to a higher standard. It is our legal right as citizens to
play a vocal part in elections, to buy property in the town where we
work, to proclaim in print the virtues of a commercial product, and,
after a year on the job (unless otherwise restricted), to leave one
position for a better-paying one. But, as true professionals, we agree
not to exercise our legal rights to the limit and not to think only of
our self-interest, but rather to give priority to the interest of our
ultimate client—the citizens of our community.

This article presents several examples of ethical problems that
confront the profession today. It is important to note that the Committee on Professional Conduct was increasingly aware of, and uncomfortable about, the unrealistic expectation that the Code in its
entirety should apply to all ICMA members—even if they are, for
example, elected officials, consultants, commercial vendors, or some
other type of private citizen. In revising the Rules of Procedure, the
Executive Board decided that affiliate members and corporate
members not in local government service should be subject only to
the First and Third Tenets.

Acceptance and
retention of appointments

Most people assume that if they're offered a job and they accept it,
they simply arrive and begin work, and that's that until at least a
couple of years later. There have been cases, however, where members have applied for two positions at the same time (no problem,
legally or ethically), accepted one, and then gone to the other at a
higher salary. There have even been cases where a member has accepted travel or moving expenses, actually started one job, and then
left for the other when it was offered. When that sort of thing occurs, the whole profession suffers.

The Committee on Professional Conduct has become tired of
explanations alleging ambiguity in the terms of appointment or
claiming that the acceptance had not yet been put in written form.
The *Guidelines on Appointment Commitment* to the Third Tenet now
states that "oral acceptance of an employment offer is considered
binding unless the employer makes fundamental changes in the
terms of employment."

Similarly, the Committee is unlikely to be impressed by the argument, made last year by a member, that the city's financial condi-

tion was not what he had expected. Unless information has been concealed, anyone holding membership in ICMA is responsible for finding out all the circumstances basic to accepting a new position.

As the *Guideline on Length of Service* to the Fourth Tenet explains, "a minimum of two years generally is considered necessary in order to render a professional service to the municipality." It is recognized, of course, that circumstances ranging from loss of confidence in the member to refusal of the appointing authority to honor commitments may justify a separation within less than two years. But as the Guideline puts it, "a short tenure should be the exception rather than a recurring experience." And once again it emphasizes that failure to check out fully the conditions or terms of employment is not one of the justifications for such an exception.

Endorsements

It is obvious that members don't like to see colleagues "pushing" commercial products, for they are quick to inform the Committee on Professional Conduct if they see an example of such behavior. Although the *Guideline on Endorsements* to the Twelfth Tenet makes it plain that endorsing a commercial product in a paid advertisement by quotation or the use of a picture is not acceptable—whether or not compensation is involved—times change, and the Guideline has now been amended. The amended Guideline excludes endorsements when they are for a public purpose, when they are directed by the governing body, and when the member receives no compensation. Examples might involve a new hotel whose development is the result of a partnership or agreement between a city or county and a private firm, or a training program for local officials presented by a council of governments.

There have been occasions when a commercial vendor has quoted an ICMA member in an advertisement without the latter's prior knowledge. If this should happen to you, do what others before you have done: call the vendor and ask that the statement be withdrawn; follow up immediately with a letter, and send the Committee on Professional Conduct a copy.

Investments

Perhaps, in a way, we should be pleased that the Committee on Professional Conduct finds it necessary nowadays to be vigilant against investments that reveal or suggest a conflict of interest. When the Code was originally framed, I doubt whether many ICMA members expected to have any substantial disposable income. And if they did, the Depression soon gave their hopes an unpleasant jolt.

Six decades later, it's still true that if you sincerely want to be rich, you don't become a city or county manager, a COG director, or an assistant. But it's also obvious that everyone's real income is far higher nowadays, and that two-career families have helped to bring about expenditure options that didn't exist a generation or two ago. We have seen, therefore, an increase in the number of complaints, and thankfully, inquiries about real estate investments and partnerships.

Neither the Twelfth Tenet of the Code nor its *Guideline on Investments in Conflict with Official Duties* flat out forbids local investments by ICMA members. But the Guideline does indicate that there should be no transaction that creates a conflict with official duties. And the *Guideline on Public Confidence* to the Third Tenet speaks of members' conduct that will "maintain public confidence in their performance of the public trust." It takes little imagination to see how the news media and the public would gain the wrong impression from a manager's purchase of real estate that at some point might involve the services of building inspectors or other local officials. Even the purchase of property far away from your jurisdiction can get you in trouble, for example, if you do it through a partnership involving other employees whose salaries you control or influence. When complaints are made, each case is judged on its own merits. A member would be wise to disclose to the governing body all investments, including those of a spouse. The greatest degree of safety lies in doing what many managers do: in the community where they work, they purchase only their own home.

Politics

The Association has always believed that a reputation for fairness and impartiality is the hallmark of the professional local government manager. The Seventh Tenet of the Code prohibits involvement not only in electing the member's legislative body, but also in other political activities that would impair the member's effectiveness.

Obviously you shouldn't take part in the elections for your board or council. But suppose the councilmember for whom you have the greatest respect is going to run for the state legislature or for Congress? The Seventh Tenet's *Guideline on Other Elections* makes it plain that ICMA members have the right to vote and to express their opinions on public matters. "However, in order not to impair their effectiveness on behalf of the municipalities they serve, they should not participate in election campaigns for representatives from their area to county, school, state, and federal offices." The reason is simple: as the Guideline implies, if your candidate doesn't win, the person who does may one day feel less than objective if you seek assistance on your jurisdiction's behalf. But beyond that, your involvement may permanently harm your professional reputation for impartiality. For both of these reasons, I believe the Committee on Professional Conduct would regard with disfavor even participation in the election of a state legislator from another district.

Certain kinds of election activities are in order, however, as the Seventh Tenet's *Guidelines on Elections on the Council-Manager Plan* and *on Presentation of Issues* indicate. It is acceptable to prepare or present materials on the Plan (even in another community, if requested), and to assist one's governing body in presenting referendum matters, such as annexations and bond issues.

Résumés

The problem of the inaccurate or incomplete résumé has been around for a long time—in all trades and professions—and the growing emphasis on paper qualifications has certainly done nothing to reduce it. A member may consider the school of hard knocks as good as Knox College and may award himself an appropriate degree. Or he or she may regard an experience with a particular local government as so unfortunate that no one else needs to know about it. Members whose cases were recently heard before the Committee on Professional Conduct have included one who cynically chose which parts of his background to reveal to prospective employers, and another, with an otherwise exemplary career behind him, who had awarded himself a degree many years earlier and lived with that uncomfortable knowledge for much of his life.

The *Guideline on Credentials* to the Third Tenet is pretty clear. It says: "An application for employment should be complete and accurate as to all pertinent details of education, experience, and personal history. Members should recognize that both omissions and inaccuracies must be avoided."

Travel expenses

ICMA members seem to be traveling more. Perhaps that's why attendance at the annual conference is up. Maybe it's also why there seem to be more unfortunate incidents with expense accounts. Complaints about members have involved amounts of money ranging from a few dollars to tens of thousands. Penalties have included expulsion from the Association as well as other actions imposed by courts of law.

The writers of the first Code of Ethics probably did not envision the coming of the credit card. Just as on a personal basis it has not helped the lives of those with the least self-control, so on an official basis it has occasionally proved tempting to those who consider themselves unjustly underpaid. If you belong to the latter category, I would strongly urge you not to fight your battles via an expense account. At some point everything will come to light.

After the countless hours of unpaid and unnoticed overtime you've devoted to the public service, it may seem simple—and harmless—enough to do what one member did and, on a conference visit far from home, add an extra digit or two to the stub from the hotel restaurant or bar. But if a local reporter decides to check out city hall expense accounts and make a phone call to that far-away hotel—as one reporter actually did—would you feel confident about explaining yourself to an ICMA fact-finding committee, keeping your job, appearing in court, or facing yourself in the mirror?

Two-career couples

The original framers of the Code of Ethics lived in a society where dad went to work and mom stayed home to look after the three or four children (not to mention dad). Sixty-three years later, women manage communities of up to a million and a half people, and those who are married to managers often have careers of their own in legal or planning firms, as well as in many other professions. A typical question that arises nowadays is that posed not long ago by a city manager who asked if there were any steps he should take now that his wife had a new law practice in the city and might have a direct or indirect interest in issues before the council. The advice of the Committee on Professional Conduct was that the manager should disclose his wife's employment to the council, and that she should avoid any direct presentation of a client's interest to the council.

The Twelfth Tenet's *Guideline on Personal Relationships* recently approved by the Executive Board states explicitly that "members should disclose any personal relationship to the governing body in any instance where there could be the appearance of a conflict of interest." Although the particular example given there is that of a spouse working for a developer doing business with a local government, the Committee on Professional Conduct wishes it to be understood that "any personal relationship" would include that of a parent or son or daughter or other close relative or close friend. As the *Guideline on Impression of Influence* to the Third Tenet makes plain, "members should conduct their official and personal affairs in such a manner as to give the clear impression that they cannot be improperly influenced in the performance of their official duties." In other words, if it wouldn't look good "revealed" to the local news media, either disclose it up front or don't do it.

Allegiance to the Code

Aristotle said that people in government exercise a teaching function. A good argument can be made that the ethical tone of a community—national, state, or local—is to a substantial degree set by people in leading government positions. For two generations, ICMA's Code of Ethics has conveyed that message. As times change, the Code, the Guidelines, and the Rules of Procedure have changed too. But one thing has remained constant: the Code is a firm statement made by a proud profession.

All of us owe allegiance to the Code—we undertake that when we join the Association. Yet, unfortunately, the record shows that occasionally there are members who deliberately act unethically (even criminally), as well as those who just don't recall what the Code and the Guidelines spell out. As my former associate on the Committee on Professional Conduct, G. Curtis Branscome, city manager of Decatur, Georgia, wrote in the January 1986 issue of *Public Management,* "Your colleagues take this business seriously. There are a number of letters in the file that say 'he is a friend and a good manager, but I think this should be investigated.'"

Ethics and Investments

_____ Elizabeth K. Kellar

A city manager wanted to invest in real estate with two of his staff. They knew they should avoid investments in the community where they worked, so they bought property in a resort area 200 miles away. Six months later, the city manager found himself the focus of headlines implying that he had a conflict of interest.

What happened? A candidate for city council read the manager's financial disclosure sheet and saw an opportunity for publicity. She could accuse the manager of favoritism because he determined salary increases for the two employees. The manager sold his share in the partnership for a small loss, and his ethics were subjected to several weeks of media scrutiny.

This incident shows that investments can be very sensitive for those in the public sector. Public sector managers need to go far beyond what is legal if they want to avoid the perception of a conflict of interest. Whenever managers are considering making an investment, they should imagine how it would look on the front page of the local newspaper.

Some public sector managers argue that it is not fair to deny themselves a golden investment opportunity. The reality is, however, that they may lose their jobs or damage their reputations if they do not carefully consider the public perceptions of their actions. When those consequences are considered, most managers are willing to make some adjustments in where or how they invest.

Reprinted with permission from _Personal Financial Planning for Local Government Employees_, edited by Bruce K. Blaylock and Kenneth F. Kennedy (Washington, D.C.: International City Management Association and ICMA Retirement Corporation, 1987).

Seek no favor

The ICMA Code of Ethics, adopted in 1924, is recognized nationally for its emphasis on the social responsibilities of those who work in local government. O.E. Carr, ICMA president in 1916 and chairman of the first ethics committee, compared ICMA's Code of Ethics with others:

From various insights which I have had into the code of ethics of the legal profession, I was inclined to think they had rules of etiquette and had to deal with the contact of one man in that profession with other men of the profession, rather than the public.[1]

The ICMA Code of Ethics has been amended five times and now includes written guidelines to interpret its 12 tenets as well as formal rules of procedure for conducting ethics investigations. ICMA encourages its members to contact the Association for advisory opinions on ethics matters. The basic purpose of the code, however, is the same today as it was in 1924; to remind local government managers of their responsibilities to citizens, to elected officials, and to their colleagues.

One of the key tenets of the ICMA Code of Ethics deals in some detail with investment questions: "Seek no favor; believe that personal aggrandizement or profit secured by confidential information or by misuse of public time is dishonest." Two guidelines for this tenet provide practical advice to ICMA members: one discusses investments that may conflict with official duties and the other warns against the use of confidential information.

Investments in Conflict with Official Duties. Members should not invest or hold any investment, directly or indirectly, in any financial business, commercial, or other private transaction which creates a conflict with their official duties.

In the case of real estate, the possibility of the use of confidential information and knowledge to further a member's personal interest requires special consideration. This guideline recognizes that a member's official actions and decisions can be influenced if there is a conflict with their personal investments. Purchases and sales which might be interpreted as speculation for quick profit ought to be avoided. The appearance that confidential information has been used to further their personal interest (as in section headed "Confidential Information" below) is a special possibility for a member in the case of real estate.

Recognizing that personal investments may prejudice or may appear to influence official actions and decisions, members may, in concert with their governing body, provide for disclosure of such investments prior to the acceptance of their position as municipal administrator or prior to any official action by the governing body that may affect such investments.

Confidential Information. Members should not disclose to others, or use to further their personal interests, confidential information acquired by them in the course of their official duties.[2]

Ethics complaints regarding investments have grown in recent years. Complaints of this nature are treated seriously by the ICMA Committee on Professional Conduct and often involve public censure or expulsion from the Association.

One member was expelled for serving as the supervisor for a building construction project in his community. Not only did this manager fail to disclose his outside employment to the city council, but he did much of the work on city time. He also pressured one of his building officials to prematurely approve inspection of this project. Later, several defects in the building were found, and the owner filed suit.

Another member was censured for failing to disclose in a timely way that he had made an investment in his community. The investment came to light when the city council had to review a zoning question on the property. The manager found himself trying to explain why he had made such an investment and why he had not informed the council. Although he immediately sold his investment share and publicly apologized, the controversy cost him his job.

There are, nevertheless, managers who hold investments in their community who have not faced charges of conflict of interest. Some might have worked in the private sector before becoming a city or county manager; they might already own investment properties and feel that they need not sell them just because they have taken a public sector job. If they fully disclose their investments to the governing body and disqualify themselves from any recommendations related to the properties, they may avoid any ethics charges.

Questions of ethical investments do not have clear answers and are the subject of much debate in the local government profession. Most people would agree, however, that the safest policy is for a manager to invest outside the community in which he or she is employed. It is equally important for a manager to disclose fully to the governing body any existing investments as well as any new investments.

Appearances count

In the fishbowl environment of the public sector, managers and other public servants are held to a much higher standard than the average citizen. While a manager may have honorable intentions, problems may surface in a variety of surprising ways. Here are a few concerns for a manager to watch for before making an investment.

Location, location   Remember the famous saying in real estate: "Always buy location, location, location." Many managers make it a practice to purchase nothing but their own homes in the communities where they work. This approach certainly minimizes the possibility of a conflict of interest charge.

Nature of investment   Be wary of "get rich quick" investment schemes that involve newly established organizations. These organizations may want to use a manager's good reputation as a front for illegal as well as unethical activities. Guilt by association can be hard to avoid, even if the manager was unaware of the organization's tactics or actions.

Similarly, in making investments on their own, managers need to consider whether they can take the time to supervise the business or property. Suppose, for example, a manager purchased a rental property in a low-income neighborhood in an adjacent community. If substandard conditions existed and were not promptly corrected, the manager could find himself the subject of an unpleasant media inquiry.

Families and friends   Even if a manager's personal investments are above reproach, his or her spouse may have questionable holdings. The obvious first step is to disclose any investment that could create an appearance of a conflict of interest. Similarly, managers should remove themselves from zoning debates or any other discussions involving holdings by their immediate families or others obviously close to them.

Managers also need to be careful about financial dealings with their employees. A county manager was expelled from ICMA because he had made false statements on a loan application. One fact he failed to disclose was a $15,000 loan from one of his subordinates.

Legal vs. ethical   Some managers assure themselves that they have acted properly if an attorney has approved an action, not realizing that public servants must distinguish between legal actions and ethical actions. This is illustrated by the case of a city manager who took advantage of a low-interest loan for the purchase of his home, which happened to be located in a census tract that qualified for a low-interest loan. As city manager, he knew that a considerable amount of money was still available for the loans and that the money was unlikely to be used up by lower-income residents. He checked with an attorney who assured him it was perfectly legal to apply for a loan himself.

The attorney had little to say, however, when the story broke in the press about how the highest-paid city official had taken advantage of a program meant for low-income residents. The manager did what he could to repair the damage to his reputation by quickly refinancing the loan.

Confidential information   By the nature of their jobs, local government employees have access to confidential information. While it may be tempting to act on information that is not yet public, it is unethical (and may be illegal) to do so.

One manager and two council members took advantage of confidential information to invest in real estate just outside the city limits. A short time later, the land was annexed to the city. The land went up in value, the public took notice, and the manager was expelled from ICMA.

Parting advice

Most local government managers who have become embroiled in controversies related to their investments had no intention of doing anything unethical. Very often their mistake was the result of poor judgment or ignorance. The following guidelines, admittedly conservative, may help managers avoid most ethics questions regarding their investments:

1.   Know the law governing conflicts of interest. When in doubt, check with the city or county attorney.
2.   Restrict real property ownership in your city or county to your own house. Be careful about making real property investments outside your city or county, especially when the properties are contiguous or adjacent to the city or county boundaries.
3.   Do not invest in businesses or other enterprises in the city or county where you work.
4.   Disclose information on your personal and family investments fully and in a timely way.
5.   Beware of rationalizations. Even if you believe you are serving your community by spending your personal time and money to invest in your community, the public may interpret your actions differently. In their eyes, you may be personally profiting from inside information gathered as a local government employee.
6.   Avoid investment partnerships with either employees or members of your governing bodies. These partnerships inevitably lead to public criticism.
7.   Consider whether or not a proposed investment will meet the standards of your professional peers. When in doubt, look elsewhere.

Notes

1. William E. Besuden, "The Profession's Heritage: The ICMA Code of Ethics," *Public Management*, March 1981, p. 3.

2. "ICMA Code of Ethics with Guidelines," *Public Management*, February 1984, p. 11.

Appendix A:
ASPA
Code of Ethics and
Implementation
Guidelines

Demonstrate the highest standards of personal integrity, truthfulness, honesty and fortitude in all our public activities in order to inspire public confidence and trust in public institutions.

Perceptions of others are critical to the reputation of an individual or a public agency. Nothing is more important to public administrators than the public's opinion about their honesty, truthfulness, and personal integrity. It overshadows competence as the premier value sought by citizens in their public officials and employees. Any individual or collective compromise with respect to these character traits can damage the ability of an agency to perform its tasks or accomplish its mission. The reputation of the administrator may be tarnished. Effectiveness may be impaired. A career or careers may be destroyed. The best insurance against loss of public confidence is adherence to the highest standards of honesty, truthfulness and fortitude.

Public administrators are obliged to develop civic virtues because of the public responsibilities they have sought and obtained. Respect for the truth, for fairly dealing with others, for sensitivity to rights and responsibilities of citizens, and for the public good must be generated and carefully nurtured and matured.

If you are responsible for the performance of others, share with them the reasons for the importance of integrity. Hold them to high ethical standards and teach them the moral as well as the financial responsibility for public funds under their care.

If you are responsible only for your own performance, do not compromise your honesty and integrity for advancement, honors, or personal gain. Be discreet, respectful of proper authority and your appointed or elected superiors, sensitive to the expectations and the values of the public you serve. Practice the golden rule: doing to and for others what you would have done to and for you in similar circumstances. Be modest about your talents, letting your work speak for you. Be generous in your praise of the good work of your fellow workers. Guard the public purse as if it were your own.

Whether you are an official or an employee, by your own example give testimony to your regard for the rights of others. Acknowledge their legitimate responsibilities, and don't trespass upon them. Concede gracefully, quickly, and publicly when you have erred. Be fair and sensitive to those who have not fared well in their dealings with your agency and its applications of the law, regulations, or administrative procedures.

Serve in such a way that we do not realize undue personal gain from the performance of our official duties.

The only gains you should seek from public employment are salaries, fringe benefits, respect, and recognition for your work. Your personal gains may also include the pleasure of doing a good job, helping the public, and achieving your career goals. No elected or appointed public servant should borrow or accept gifts from staff of any corporation which buys services from, or sells to, or is regulated by, his or her governmental agency. If your work brings you in frequent contact with contractors supplying the government, be sure you pay for your own expenses. Public property, funds and power should never be directed toward personal or political gain. Make it clear by your own actions that you will not tolerate any use of public funds to benefit yourself, your family, or your friends.

Avoid any interest or activity which is in conflict with the conduct of our official duties.

Public employees should not undertake any task which is in conflict or could be viewed as in conflict with job responsibilities.

This general statement addresses a fundamental principle that public employees are trustees for all the people. This means that the people have a right to expect public employees to act as surrogates for the entire people with fairness toward all the people and not a few or a limited group.

Actions or inactions which conflict with, injure, or destroy this foundation of trust between the people and their surrogates must be avoided.

Ironically, experience indicates that conflict of interest and corruption often arise not from an external affront, but as a result of interaction between persons who know each other very well. To strengthen resistance to conflict of interest, public employees should avoid frequent social contact with persons who come under their regulation or persons who wish to sell products or services to their agency or institution.

Agencies with inspectional or investigative responsibilities have a special obligation to reduce vulnerability to conflict of interest. Periodic staff rotation may be helpful to these agencies.

Individuals holding a position recognized by law or regulation as an unclassified or political appointment (e.g., Cabinet level and Governor's appointment positions) have a special obligation to behave in ways which do not suggest that official acts are driven primarily or only by partisan political concerns.

Public employees should remember that despite whatever preventive steps they might take, situations which hold the possibility for conflict of interest will always emerge. Consequently, the awareness of the potentiality of conflict of interest is important. Public employees, particularly professors in Public Administration, have a serious obligation to periodically stimulate discussion on conflicts of interest within organizations, schools, and professional associations.

Support, implement, and promote merit employment and programs of affirmative action to assure equal employment opportunity by our recruitment, selection, and advancement of qualified persons from all elements of society.

Oppose any discrimination because of race, color, religion, sex, national origin, political affiliation, physical handicaps, age, or marital status, in all aspects of personnel policy. Likewise, a person's lifestyle should not be the occasion for discrimination if it bears no reasonable relation to his or her ability to perform required tasks.

Review employment and personnel operations and statistics to identify the impact of organizational practices on "protected groups." Performance standards should apply equally to all workers. In the event of cutbacks of staff, managers should employ fair criteria for selection of employees for separation, and humane strategies for administrating the program.

Any kind of sexual, racial, or religious harassment should not be allowed. Appropriate channels should be provided for harassed persons to state their problems to objective officials. In the event of a proven offense, appropriate action should be taken.

Eliminate all forms of illegal discrimination, fraud, and mis-management of public funds, and support colleagues if they are in difficulty because of responsible efforts to correct such discrimination, fraud, mismanagement or abuse.

If you are a supervisor, you should not only be alert that no illegal action issues from or is sponsored by your immediate office, you should inform your subordinates at regular intervals that you will tolerate no illegalities in their offices and discuss the reasons for the position with them. Public employees who have good reason to suspect illegal action in any public agency should seek assistance in how to channel the information regarding the matter to appropriate authorities.

All public servants should support authorized investigative agencies, the General Accounting Office in the federal government, auditors in the state or large local governments, C.P.A. firms or federal or state auditors in many other cases. We should support the concept of independent auditors reporting to committees independent of management. Good fiscal and management controls and inspections are important protections for supervisors, staff, and the public interest.

In both government and business, inadequate equipment, software, procedures, supervision, and poor security controls make possible both intentional and unintentional misconduct. Managers have an ethical obligation to seek adequate equipment, software, procedures and controls to reduce the agency's vulnerability to misconduct. When an agency dispenses exemptions from regulations, or abatement of taxes or fees, managers should assure periodic investigatory checks.

The "whistle blower" who appears to his/her immediate superiors to be disloyal, may actually be loyal to the higher interests of the public. If so, the whistle blower deserves support. Local, state, and federal governments should establish effective dissent channels to which whistle blowers may report their concerns without fear of identification.

Supervisors should inform their staff that constructive criticism may be brought to them without reprisal, or may be carried to an ombudsman or other designated official. As a last resort, public employees have a right to make public their criticism but it is the personal and professional responsibility of the critic to advance only well-founded criticism.

Serve the public with respect, concern, courtesy, and responsiveness, recognizing that service to the public is beyond service to oneself.

Be sure your answers to questions on public policy are complete, understandable and true. Try to develop in your staff a goal of courteous conduct with citizens. Devise a simple system to ensure that your staff gives helpful and pleasant service to the public. Wherever possible, show citizens how to avoid mistakes in their relations with government.

Each citizen's questions should be answered as thoughtfully and as fully as possible. If you or your staff do not know the answer to a question, an effort should be made to get an answer or to help the citizen make direct contact with the appropriate office.

Part of servicing the public responsively is to encourage citizen cooperation and to involve civic groups. Administrators have an ethical responsibility to bring citizens into work with the government as far as practical, both to secure citizen support of government, and for the economics or increased effectiveness which will result. Respect the right of the public (through the media) to know what is going on in your agency even though you know queries may be raised for partisan or other non-public purposes.

Strive for personal professional excellence and encourage the professional development of our associates and those seeking to enter the field of public administration.

Staff members, throughout their careers, should be encouraged to participate in professional activities and associations such as ASPA. They should also be reminded of the importance of doing a good job and their responsibility to improve the public service.

Administrators should make time to meet with students periodically and to provide a bridge between classroom studies and the realities of public jobs. Administrators should also lend their support to well planned internship programs.

Approach our organization and operational duties with a positive attitude and constructively support open communication, creativity, dedication and compassion.

Americans expect government to be compassionate, well organized, and operating within the law. Public employees should understand the purpose of their agency and the role they play in achieving that purpose. Dedication and creativity of staff members will flow from a sense of purpose.

ASPA members should strive to create a work environment which supports positive and constructive attitudes among workers at all levels. This open environment should permit employees to comment on work activities without fear of reprisal. In addition, managers can strengthen this open environment by establishing procedures ensuring thoughtful and objective review of employee concerns.

Respect and protect the privileged information to which we have access in the course of official duties.

Much information in public offices is privileged for reasons of national security, or because of laws or ordinances. If you talk with colleagues about privileged matters, be sure they need the information and you enjoin them to secrecy. If the work is important enough to be classified, learn and follow the rules set by the security agency. Special care must be taken to secure access to confidential information stored on computers. Sometimes information needs to be withheld from the individual citizen or general public to prevent disturbances of the peace. It should be withheld only if there is a possibility of dangerous or illegal or unprofessional consequences of releasing information.

Where other governmental agencies have a legitimate public service need for information possessed by an agency, do all you can to cooperate, within the limits of statute law, administrative regulations, and promises made to those who furnish the information.

Exercise whatever discretionary authority we have under law to promote the public interest.

If your work involves discretionary decisions you should first secure policy guidelines from your supervisor. You should then make sure that all staff who "need to know" are informed of these policies and have an opportunity to discuss the means of putting them into effect.

There are occasions when a law is unenforceable or has become obsolete; in such cases you should recommend to your superior or the legislative body that the law be modernized. If an obsolete law remains in effect, the manager or highest official should determine if the law is or is not be enforced, after consultation with the agency's legal advisor.

There are occasions where a lower level employee must be given considerable discretion. Try to see that such employees are adequately trained for their difficult tasks.

Tell yourself and your staff quite frequently that every decision creates a precedent, so the first decisions on a point should be ethically sound; this is the best protection for staff as well as for the public.

Accept as a personal duty the responsibility to keep up to date on emerging issues and to administer the public's business with professional competence, fairness, impartiality, efficiency and effectiveness.

Administrators should attend professional meetings, read books and periodicals related to their field, and talk with specialists. The goal is to keep informed about the present and future issues and problems in their professional field and organization in order to take advantage of opportunities and avoid problems.

Serious mistakes in public administration have been made by people who did their jobs conscientiously but failed to look ahead for emerging problems and issues. A long list of washed out dams, fatal mine accidents, fires in poorly inspected buildings, inadequate computer systems, or economic disasters are results of not looking ahead. ASPA members should be catalysts to stimulate discussion and reflection about improving efficiency and effectiveness of public services.

Respect, support, study, and when necessary, work to improve federal and state constitutions and other laws which define the relationships among public agencies, employees, clients and all citizens.

Familiarize yourself with principles of American constitutional government. As a citizen work for legislation which is in the public interest.

Teach constitutional principles of equality and fairness.

Strive for clear division of functions between different levels of government, between different bureaus or departments, and between government and its citizens. Cooperate as fully as possible with all agencies of government, especially those with overlapping responsibilities. Do not let parochial agency or institutional loyalty drown out considerations of wider public policy.

Adopted by
ASPA National Council
March 27, 1985

Appendix B: ICMA Code of Ethics with Guidelines

1. Be dedicated to the concepts of effective and democratic local government by responsible elected officials and believe that professional general management is essential to the achievement of this objective.

2. Affirm the dignity and worth of the services rendered by government and maintain a constructive, creative, and practical attitude toward urban affairs and a deep sense of social responsibility as a trusted public servant.

Guideline

Advice to officials of other municipalities When members advise and respond to inquiries from elected or appointed officials of other municipalities, they should inform the administrators of those communities.

3. Be dedicated to the highest ideals of honor and integrity in all public and personal relationships in order that the member may merit the respect and confidence of the elected officials, of other officials and employees, and of the public.

Guidelines

Public confidence Members should conduct themselves so as to maintain public confidence in their profession, their local government, and in their performance of the public trust.

Impression of influence Members should conduct their official and personal affairs in such a manner so as to give the clear impression that they cannot be improperly influenced in the performance of their official duties.

Appointment commitment Members who accept an appointment to a position should not fail to report for that position. This does not preclude the possibility of a member considering several offers or seeking several positions at the same time, but once a bona fide offer of a position has been accepted, that commitment should be honored. Oral acceptance of an employment offer is considered binding unless the employer makes fundamental changes in the terms of employment.

Credentials   An application for employment should be complete and accurate as to all pertinent details of education, experience, and personal history. Members should recognize that both omission and inaccuracies must be avoided.

Professional respect   Members seeking a management position should show professional respect for persons formerly holding the position or for others who might be applying for the same position. Professional respect does not preclude honest differences of opinion; it does preclude attacking a person's motives or integrity in order to be appointed to a position.

Confidentiality   Members should not discuss or divulge information with anyone about pending or completed ethics cases, except as specifically authorized by the Rules of Procedure for Enforcement of the Code of Ethics.

Seeking employment   Members should not seek employment in a community having an incumbent administrator who has not resigned or been officially informed that his or her services are to be terminated.

4.   Recognize that the chief function of local government at all times is to serve the best interests of all of the people.

Guideline

Length of service   A minimum of two years generally is considered necessary in order to render a professional service to the municipality. A short tenure should be the exception rather than a recurring experience. However, under special circumstances it may be in the best interests of the municipality and the member to separate in a shorter time. Examples of such circumstances would include a refusal of the appointing authority to honor commitments concerning conditions of employment, a vote of no confidence in the member, or severe personal problems. It is the responsibility of an applicant for a position to ascertain conditions of employment. Inadequately determining terms of employment prior to arrival does not justify premature termination.

5.   Submit policy proposals to elected officials; provide them with facts and advice on matters of policy as a basis for making decisions and setting community goals, and uphold and implement municipal policies adopted by elected officials.

Guideline

Conflicting roles   Members who serve multiple roles—working as both city attorney and city manager for the same community, for example—should avoid participating in matters that create the appearance of a conflict of interest. They should disclose the potential conflict to the governing body so that other opinions may be solicited.

6.   Recognize that elected representatives of the people are entitled to the credit for the establishment of municipal policies; responsibility for public execution rests with the members.

7.   Refrain from participation in the election of the members of the employing legislative body, and from all partisan political activities which would impair performance as a professional administrator.

Guidelines

Elections of the governing body Members should maintain a reputation for serving equally and impartially all members of the governing body of the municipality they serve, regardless of party. To this end, they should not engage in active participation in the election campaign on behalf of or in opposition to candidates for the governing body.

Other elections Members share with their fellow citizens the right and responsibility to exercise their franchise and voice their opinion on public issues. However, in order not to impair their effectiveness on behalf of the municipalities they serve, they should not participate in election campaigns for representatives from their area to county, school, state, and federal offices.

Elections on the council-manager plan Members may assist in preparing and presenting materials that explain the council-manager form of government to the public prior to an election on the use of the plan. If assistance is required by another community, members may respond. All activities regarding ballot issues should be conducted within local regulations and in a professional manner.

Presentation of issues Members may assist the governing body in presenting issues involved in referenda such as bond issues, annexations, and similar matters.

8. Make it a duty continually to improve the member's professional ability and to develop the competence of associates in the use of management techniques.

9. Keep the community informed on municipal affairs; encourage communication between the citizens and all municipal officers; emphasize friendly and courteous service to the public; and seek to improve the quality and image of public service.

10. Resist any encroachment on professional responsibilities, believing the member should be free to carry out official policies without interference, and handle each problem without discrimination on the basis of principle and justice.

Guideline

Information sharing The member should openly share information with the governing body while diligently carrying out the member's responsibilities as set forth in the charter or enabling legislation.

11. Handle all matters of personnel on the basis of merit so that fairness and impartiality govern a member's decisions, pertaining to appointments, pay adjustments, promotions, and discipline.

Guideline

Equal opportunity Members should develop a positive program that will ensure meaningful employment opportunities for all segments of the community. All programs, practices, and operations should: (1) provide equality of opportunity in employment for all persons; (2) prohibit discrimination because of race, color, religion, sex, national origin, political affiliation, physical handicaps, age, or marital status; and (3) promote continuing programs of affirmative action at every level within the organization.

It should be the member's personal and professional responsibility to actively recruit and hire minorities and women to serve on professional staffs throughout their organization.

12.   Seek no favor; believe that personal aggrandizement or profit secured by confidential information or by misuse of public time is dishonest.

Guidelines
Gifts Members should not directly or indirectly solicit any gift or accept or receive any gift—whether it be money, services, loan, travel, entertainment, hospitality, promise, or any other form—under the following circumstances: (1) it could reasonably be inferred or expected that the gift was intended to influence them in the performance of their official duties; or (2) the gift was intended to serve as a reward for any official action on their part.

It is important that the prohibition of unsolicited gifts be limited to circumstances related to improper influence. In de minimus situations such as tobacco and meal checks for example, some modest maximum dollar value should be determined by the member as a guideline. The guideline is not intended to isolate members from normal social practices where gifts among friends, associates, and relatives are appropriate for certain occasions.

Investments in conflict with official duties Members should not invest or hold any investment, directly or indirectly, in any financial business, commercial, or other private transaction that creates a conflict with their official duties.

In the case of real estate, the potential use of confidential information

and knowledge to further a member's personal interest requires special consideration. This guideline recognizes that members' official actions and decisions be be influenced if there is a conflict with personal investments. Purchases and sales which might be interpreted as speculation for quick profit ought to be avoided (see the section below on "Confidential Information").

Because personal investments may prejudice or may appear to influence official actions and decisions, members may, in concert with their governing body, provide for disclosure of such investments prior to accepting their position as municipal administrator or prior to any official action by the governing body that may affect such investments.

Personal relationships Members should disclose any personal relationship to the governing body in any instance where there could be the appearance of a conflict of interest. For example, if the manager's spouse works for a developer doing business with the local government, that fact should be disclosed.

Confidential information Members should not disclose to others, or use to further their personal interest, confidential information acquired by them in the course of their official duties.

Private employment Members should not engage in, solicit, negotiate for, or promise to accept private employment nor should they render services for private interests or conduct a private business when such employment, service, or business creates a conflict with or impairs the proper discharge of their official duties.

Teaching, lecturing, writing, or consulting are typical activities that may not involve conflict of interest or impair the proper discharge of their official duties. Prior notification of the governing body is appropriate in all cases of outside employment.

Representation Members should not represent any outside interest before an agency, whether public or private, except with the authorization of or at the direction of the legislative body of the governmental unit they serve.

Endorsement Members should not endorse commercial products by agreeing to use their photograph, endorsement, or quotation in paid advertisements, unless the endorse-

ment is for a public purpose, is directed by the governing body, and the member receives no compensation. Examples of public purposes include economic development for the local government and the sale of local government products.

Members' observations, opinions, and analyses of commercial products used or tested by their municipalities are appropriate and useful to the profession when included as a part of professional articles and reports.

As adopted by
The ICMA Executive Board
May 1987

Appendix C: For Further Reference

Appleby, Paul H. *Morality and Administration in Democratic Government.* Baton Rouge: Louisiana State University Press, 1952.

Barnard, Chester. "The Nature of Executive Responsibility." In *The Functions of the Executive,* 258–84. Cambridge: Harvard University Press, 1938.

Bowman, James S. "Whistle Blowing in the Public Sector: An Overview of the Issues." *Review of Public Personnel Administration* (Fall 1980): 15–27.

Caiden, Gerald E. "Ethics in the Public Service: Codification Misses the Target." *Public Personnel Management* 10, no. 1 (1981): 146–52.

Chandler, Ralph C. "Ethics and Public Policy." *Commonweal* 105 (12 May 1978): 302–9.

"City Management Declaration of Ideals." *Public Management* 65 (August 1984).

Cleveland, Harlan. "A Philosophy for the Public Executive." In *Perspectives on Public Management,* edited by Robert T. Golembiewski. Itasca, IL: R. E. Peacock, 1978.

Drucker, Peter. "Ethical Chic." *Forbes,* September 14, 1981, 160–173.

"Ethics." *Public Management* 66 (February 1984).

"Ethics." *Public Management* 69 (August 1987).

"Ethics: Dictates and Dilemmas." *Public Management* 63 (March 1981).

"Ethics in Local Government." *Public Management* 57 (June 1975).

Fleishman, Joel L., and Bruce L. Payne. *Ethical Dilemmas and the Education of Policymakers.* Hastings-on-Hudson, NY: The Hastings Center, 1980.

Fleishman, Joel L., Lance Leibman, and Mark H. Moore, eds. *Public Duties: The Moral Obligations of Government Officials.* Cambridge: Harvard University Press, 1981.

French, Peter A. *Ethics in Government.* Englewood Cliffs, NJ: Prentice-Hall, 1983.

Kaplan, Abraham. *American Ethics and Public Policy.* New York: Oxford University Press, 1963.

Leys, Wayne A. R. *Ethics for Policy Decisions: The Art of Asking Deliberate Questions.* New York: Prentice-Hall, 1952.

McCoy, Charles S. *Management of Values: The Ethical Difference in Corporate Policy and Performance.* Marshfield, MA: Pitman Publishing, 1985, 177–202.

Melden, A. I. *Ethical Theories: A Book of Readings.* New York: Prentice-Hall, 1955, 1–13.

Mertins, Herman Jr., and P. J. Hennigan, eds. *Applying Professional Standards and Ethics in the Eighties: A*

Workbook and Study Guide for Public Administrators. 2d ed. Washington, D.C.: American Society for Public Administration, 1982.

Monypenney, Phillip. "A Code of Ethics as a Means of Controlling Administrative Conduct." *Public Administrative Review* 13 (Summer 1953): 184-87.

Pastin, Mark. "Ethics and Excellence." *New Management* (Spring 1987): 40-3.

_____. "Management Think." *Journal of Business Ethics* 4 (1985): 297-307.

Peters, Thomas, and Robert Waterman, Jr. "Hands-on, Value Driven." In *In Search of Excellence*, 279-91. New York: Harper and Row, 1982.

Rohr, John. *Ethics for Bureaucrats: An Essay on Law and Values.* New York: Marcel Dekker, 1978.

_____. "Ethics for the Senior Executive Service: Suggestions for Management Training." *Administration and Society* 12, no. 2 (1980): 203-16.

Scott, William A. *Values and Organizations.* Chicago: Rand McNally, 1965.

Simon, Herbert A., Donald W. Smithburg, and Victor A. Thompson. "Administrative Responsibility: Formal Controls," and "Administrative Responsibility: Informal Controls." In *Public Administration.* New York: Alfred A. Knopf, 1950.

Thompson, Dennis: "Moral Responsibility of Public Officials: The Problem of Many Hands." *American Political Science Review* 74 (December 1980): 905-16.

Thompson, Dennis, and Amy Gutman, eds. *Ethics and Politics: Cases and Comments.* Chicago: Nelson-Hall, 1984.

Tong, Rosemarie. *Ethics in Policy Analysis.* Englewood Cliffs, NJ: Prentice-Hall, 1986, 62-80.

Weber, James. "Institutionalizing Ethics into the Corporation." *MSU Business Topics* (Spring 1981): 48-52.

Practical Management Series

**Ethical Insight, Ethical Action:
Perspectives for the Local Government Manager**

Text type
Century Expanded

Composition
Unicorn Graphics
Washington, D.C.

Printing and binding
R. R. Donnelley & Sons Company
Harrisonburg, Virginia

Cover design
Rebecca Geanaros